BRANDER'S GUIDE TO SCOTCH WHISKY

BRANDER'S GUIDE

TO

SCOTCH WHISKY

Michael Brander

Lyons & Burford, Publishers

To Ed Zern
Transatlantic Sportsman and Literary Critic
who assessed some fine malt whiskies with me

© 1974, 1990, 1992, 1995, 1996 by Michael Brander

ALL RIGHTS RESERVED. No part of this book may be reproduced in any manner without the express written consent of the publisher, except in the case of brief excerpts in critical reviews and articles. All inquiries should be addressed to Lyons & Burford, Publishers, 31 West 21 Street, New York, NY 10010.

Printed in the United States of America

10 9 8 7 6 5 4 3 2 1

Design by Fleuron/Holly A. Block

Library of Congress Cataloging-in-Publication Data

Brander, Michael.
Brander's guide to Scotch whisky/Michael Brander.
p. cm.
Includes bibliographical references.
ISBN 1-55821-480-1 (pbk.)
1. Whiskey—Scotland. I. Title.
TP605.B675 1996
641.2'52'09411—dc20 96-22292
CIP

CONTENTS

INTRODUCTION

In 1974 I wrote *A History of Scotch Whisky, The Original Scotch,* which gained the Glenfiddich Award to the Malt Whisky Book Author of the Year. This was followed in 1975 by *A Guide to Scotch Whisky,* published by Johnston & Bacon of Edinburgh. After numerous reprintings, this went out of print in the late 1980s only with the demise of the old established firm. Meanwhile, in 1982, I had written a short *Introduction to Scotch Whisky,* published by Holmes McDougal. In 1990 the essentials of these three books were combined in *The Essential Guide to Scotch Whisky,* published by Canongate Publishing Ltd. In 1992 a revised second edition was published by Canongate Press, which went into receivership in 1994. This new and freshly updated revised second edition of the *Guide,* which has been selling steadily over the past twenty years, is now published by the Gleneil Press, retitled, justifiably, *The Original Guide to Scotch Whisky.*

This is intended as a basic guide to anyone interested in Scotch whisky. There is a brief introduction to the origins of Scotch from the earliest days to the present, showing how the drink is essentially a product of Scotland's barley, water, and peat as well as the inherited skills of the distillers, who have passed them down through the centuries. The years when Scotch whisky was produced illegally because of crushing taxation are also briefly outlined. Then came the boom years of the last century when Scotch whisky was first sold all around the world. These were followed by the lean years of the two World Wars until finally the post-1945 period was reached. I show how foreign investment has not always been a good thing and how successive governments have damaged Scotland's greatest industry. I also show how patent-still grain whisky is made and how this differs crucially from pot-still malt distilling. I then delineate the art of the blender and from that indicate how Scotch whisky, whether blended or malt, should be drunk for maximum enjoyment and personal satisfaction (see Do-It-Yourself, pages 29–30). After this brief but illuminating introduction, in the major part of the book I go through Scotland's malt distilleries alphabetically, indicating their whereabouts, their background, their present owners, and the quality of their product. Even those who think they know their Scotch whisky will find something of value in these pages, and for those who wish to learn about Scotch whisky, here, devoid of frills but with all that anyone needs know, is the perfect pocket introduction.

Acknowledgments

My grateful thanks and acknowledgements once again are owed to very many people throughout the Scotch whisky industry for their ready and willing assistance. It is perhaps invidious to single out individuals and, understandably enough, many prefer not to be mentioned at all, but once again I must place on record how very helpful everyone whom I have approached has been, from the Scotch Whisky Association downwards. In particular I would like to thank the many un-named distillers and distillery workers who have invariably been very helpful and courteous, as well as pleasant to meet. My thanks for their assistance in finding my way through the seemingly never-ending maze of closures and takeovers are due especially to Hector MacLennan at the Dumbarton office of Allied Distillers; W. G. MacGregor at Highland Distillers; Stuart Roberton at Inver House Distillers; Jim McColl at Morrison Bowmore; Ross Gunn, Ann Miller and Libby Jones of Seagram Distillers; Ken Robertson, Jane Richardson and Elisa Ferbej in the Edinburgh offices of United Distillers; Moyra Peffer and Richard Paterson at Whyte & Mackay; Andrew McDonald and Mrs. McEwan at the Scotch Whisky Heritage Centre; and many others. I would also like to thank M. Thierry Chauvet, from Tahiti, who pointed out that in mediaeval French, aqua vitae (page 2 et seq.) meant not "water of life" as so often translated, but simply "strong, or powerful, waters," which having regard to the distilling standards of the day was more realistic. Finally, any opinions expressed are entirely my own and for any faults, omissions or mistakes I am entirely responsible.

Chapter One
The Background of Scotch Whisky

Scotland's Heritage

Scotch whisky may only legally be distilled in Scotland. Any bottles claiming to contain Scotch whisky that is not distilled in Scotland—from Very Old Black and White Horses made in Chile to Finest Rising Sun Scotch Whisky or Whisaki made in Tokyo—are illegal and the makers may be prosecuted. Scotch whisky has been made in Scotland for centuries, but regrettably the majority of Scots themselves know remarkably little about it, or about the art of distilling it. This is a part of the national heritage about which there is still a widespread and lamentable ignorance, despite efforts during the 1980s to remedy this, from the opening of distilleries as tourist attractions, to the publication of numerous books on the subject and the opening of the Scotch Whisky Heritage Centre in Edinburgh. It must be appreciated, however, that Scotch whisky distilling, especially the distilling of Scotch malt whisky in pot-stills, is not just another industry, and that Scotch whisky, especially Scotch malt whisky, is not just another drink, but that both are an integral part of Scotland itself. The pure air and water, the peat and the soil of Scotland, along with the inherited skills of the distillers themselves, combine magically in the making of Scotch whisky.

ORIGINS

The elementary fact that alcohol boils at a lower temperature than water forms the basis of all distillation. Distilling is basically nothing more than boiling fermented liquor in a container. In primitive stills the steam is led off in a long tube, or condenser, like the elongated spout of a kettle. As the steam cools it reverts to liquid again in the form of alcohol, which in such a simple still would contain lethal impurities as well. Like the invention of gunpowder, distilling probably originated in the Far East, where the process may have started with primitive stills using bamboo and heating the juice of naturally fermented fruits.

ARRIVAL IN BRITAIN

When the art of distilling first reached Britain is uncertain, but the making of ale from fermented malted barley, the first stage in the distilling of Scotch whisky, was known around the 6th century and possibly earlier. It has been suggested that St Patrick introduced the art of distilling to Scotland as early as the 5th century. Producing Scotch whisky from malted barley probably started a good deal later, possibly somewhere around the 11th or 12th century, by which time both the Scots and the Irish were undoubtedly experienced in the art of distilling spirits. It seems likely, therefore, that the Scots have known the art of distilling Scotch whisky for over a thousand years.

AQUA VITAE

In Europe, where fermented grapes in the shape of wine were readily available, the distillation of wine produced brandy, known as aqua vitae, or strong waters. In Scotland, where fermented barley was the basis for ale, then the national drink, it would have been natural enough to use this as the basis for distilling, although the lees of wine were probably used at first. The use of fermented barley would have produced the earliest Scotch whisky, but at first, like brandy, this was also termed aqua vitae. It is thus difficult to say with any certainty when fermented barley was first used in place of wine, since in those early days there were no records of the distilling process.

First Recorded Use of Malted Barley

The earliest known record of malted barley being used instead of wine to make aqua vitae is in the Scottish Exchequer Rolls dated 1494 and reads: "Eight bolls of malt to Friar John Cor, wherewith to make aqua vitae." As eight bolls amounts to half a ton of malt, enough to make around seventy gallons of aqua vitae, it may be safely assumed that this was by no means the first time that Friar John Cor, or his fellow friars, had made Scotch whisky. Although Scotch whisky had probably been produced for many years in Scottish monasteries, since the spirit was generally referred to in the early days only as aqua vitae it is not possible to say when the practice first started. It is also impossible to know when the art spread beyond the confines of the monasteries to become a purely domestic pastime.

Origins of the Name Whisky

It is as late as 1618 before the first mention may be found in an account of a chieftain's funeral in the Highlands of the drinking of *Uisge beatha*. This is Gaelic for the Water of Life and the equivalent of aqua vitae. It was natural enough by degrees simply to refer to *Uisge*. Thereafter, it was a very simple corruption of the Gaelic to arrive at the word Whisky.

The Early Distilling Process

To judge by surviving illustrations, the stills of the 15th and 16th centuries were primitive indeed. Although there are plenty of entries in the Exchequer Rolls to prove that the King of Scotland and his nobles were fond of whisky, the spirit in those days must have been not only powerful, but also potentially lethal. Without accurate instruments for measuring quality and strength, it required great skill and practice to draw off the pure *middle cut* of the spirit and avoid the *foreshots*, or oily and poisonous higher alcohols at the start, and the later *feints* or *aftershots*, containing the lower alcohols at the end of the distilling process. During the 16th and 17th centuries, the methods of distilling were steadily improved and by this time it was a normal domestic chore, but even so it was not until the 18th century that distilling became really widespread in Scotland. Although the primitive 16th-century stills probably held little more than thirty or forty gallons at most, by the mid-18th century stills holding several hundred gallons were commonplace and distilling had become both a science and an art.

Proof: The Measurement of Quality and Strength

In these early stages, gauging the quality and strength of spirit distilled was very rough and ready. One of the commoner methods was to set a measure alight and note how much was left. Another was to add a measure of gunpowder. If when lit it exploded, this was considered too strong and *over proof*, but conversely, if difficult to light it was considered weak and *under proof*. If it burned steadily it was considered the correct strength or *proof*. Then in 1675 Robert Boyle developed his instrument for comparing the specific gravities of liquids, and "Boyle's Bubble," although not accurate to a fine degree, was used to decide whether a spirit was below or above proof. It was over a hundred years before an improvement in this early hydrometer was introduced and even then it was erratic. Accurate gauging of proof was not achieved until 1818, when the government introduced a reliable hydrometer invented by an excise officer named Sikes. Under this, spirit of proof strength at 51°F weighs 12/13 of a similar quantity of distilled water.

The National Drink

Until the Union of the Parliaments in 1707 ale, not whisky, was the national drink of Scotland. Ale was more popular by far, especially in the Lowlands and with the mass of the population, than the then relatively expensive and less widely available spirit. While ale may have been the most popular drink with the bulk of the nation, the upper classes—professional men and the aristocracy—tended to drink mainly claret, then readily obtainable from France. The imposition of a tax on malt in Scotland in 1725, contrary to the terms laid down in the Act of Union, resulted initially in widespread rioting and ultimately forced the brewers to raise the price of ale to cover their costs. It soon became apparent that a comparatively simple way to avoid the tax was to distil whisky illicitly instead of making ale, and a gradual change in the public taste resulted. By the end of the 18th century, whisky had replaced ale as the national drink. There was also the interesting side effect towards the end of the 18th century that the Lowland distillers, distilling legally and paying tax on their malted barley, were forced to use quantities of unmalted barley to keep their costs down. Their whisky was thus naturally inferior to that of the Highland distillers, who paid no tax and distilled their whisky illicitly.

Early Lowland Distillers: Haig and Stein

At least one of the names subsequently to become prominent in the Scotch whisky industry had already been noted publicly in that connection as early as the latter half of the 17th century. A farming family named Haig at Throsk near Stirling were accused of distilling whisky on the Sabbath in the year 1655 and were summoned before the Kirk Session to be rebuked for their sins, but in the end their servant lass was held to blame. From the 18th century onwards the Haigs were to become one of the leading families in the developing Scotch whisky industry in the Lowlands and went on, of course, to become one of the best-known names in Scotch whisky right up to the present day. They intermarried with the Steins, another well-known Lowland distilling family of the late 18th and early 19th centuries. By the last quarter of the 18th century, Robert and John Haig at Leith and James and John Stein at Clackmannan were using stills of over a thousand gallons capacity. To avoid the malt tax they used potatoes, turnips, and other roots, or oats and wheat, for distilling, using only small quantities of malted barley to aid the fermenting process. Although this spirit was much inferior to that produced from malted barley, there was a great demand for the product in the highly populated Lowlands and they also exported it to England, where it was refined into gin, even engaging in a deliberate trade war with the gin distillers in England.

Penal Taxation: Causes and Effects

This competition from Scotland roused the anger of the powerful gin distillers' lobby in England. As a result of their pressures, the government was persuaded to introduce what amounted to punitive taxation against the Scottish whisky distillers, basing this initially on the mistaken belief that a still could only be worked once in 24 hours. Ever-increasing taxation from 1784 onwards and throughout the war with France led to ever-increasing evasion and also to desperate measures to stay within the law. Ingenious Scottish distillers successfully distilled as much as eighty gallons of whisky in 3½ minutes, but naturally this tended to damage both the stills and the standard of whisky produced. The Haigs managed to survive, but the Steins, who had engaged in a cut-throat war with the southern distillers, were forced into bankruptcy. As taxation still continued to rise under pressure from the English distillers, many Scots distillers were literally forced to turn to illegal distilling to survive.

The Highland Line

From the 1770s onwards, distilling became more and more widespread in the Highlands, but still on a much smaller scale than in the Lowlands. One of the seemingly minor pieces of legislation introduced in 1784 to simplify the taxation laws was what would become known as the Highland Line, a somewhat arbitrary line running roughly from Glasgow to Dundee. Anything north of this line was regarded as Highland and taxed at a much lesser degree than in the Lowlands. Steadily increasing taxation on whisky from 1784 led to more and more illicit distilling in the Highlands, where, unlike the Lowlands, it was still very much more a cottage industry practiced on every croft and small farm to make ends meet. Without the income from distilling whisky, it would have been impossible for the average Highland tenant farmer of this period to pay his rent.

The Shape of the Still

In the early days the stills varied very greatly in size and shape, but by the end of the 18th century they had mostly standardised into something approaching the modern form, which evolved largely because of the need to distil at a great speed to beat the taxation system. Naturally enough, the illicit stills were nothing like as elaborate as those that were legally taxed. By the late 18th century, however, there were several master coppersmiths openly advertising their wares in Inverness under the sign of a whisky still.

An Illicit Still

A simple illicit still might be made from a cauldron with a cover and a spout fitted tightly in place with tow, like a lid. The spout would lead off to a coil, or worm, a spiral of copper tubing, often enclosed in a barrel, with cold water from a nearby burn flowing through it to hasten the cooling process. With the cooling came the condensation of the spirit.

Such primitive stills could be readily moved and were usually sited in a convenient cave, or hollow, on a hillside close to a burn supplying readily available water.

The Distilling Process

Sufficient sacks of barley would be steeped in the burn for around three days before being spread out to germinate in the cave or a convenient barn. The germinating barley had to be turned every day for some ten days before being dried over a peat fire to halt the germination when it was felt to have reached the right stage. This malted barley was then placed in a mash tun, generally a large barrel, and water was poured over it. This was then stirred every few hours until the resulting mixture was drained off into another barrel and the process repeated. The liquor resulting from this process was and still is known as wort, and the product of these two soakings of the grain would then be mixed together in a larger barrel and yeast would be added to them to assist in the fermentation. The resulting liquid, known as low wash, would then be heated and put through the still and became transformed into low wines. The still had then to be thoroughly cleaned before the low wines were put through it again, with the end result finally becoming malt whisky. This method, greatly refined and using two separate pot-stills, is more or less how malt whisky is produced today.

The Act of 1823

In 1823, after a Board of Trade Commission had reported on the facts to Parliament, a reforming act to eliminate illegal distilling was introduced with the support of the Duke of Gordon. A flat rate of £10 was introduced on all stills of forty gallons upwards and a duty of 2s 3d placed on each gallon of spirits distilled. Encouraged by the Duke of Gordon, one of the first to take advantage of the new act was George Smith in Glenlivet, despite threats from his neighbours to burn down his distillery.

The Effect of the Act of 1823

The immediate result was that within two years the amount of tax-paid whisky had increased from two million to six million gallons annually. The long-term effect was to change what had amounted to little more than a cottage craft into a considerable industry that by the end of the century was to become one of Scotland's principal assets. The results of too-high taxation on the industry are something that should still be borne in mind and it may be argued that this stage has already been reached and passed with as dire effects on the industry today as in 1820.

Pot-Still Distilling: First Stage

The method of producing malt whisky by pot-still distillation was by this time well developed. The best available Scottish barley was transported to the distillery by pack-horse, cart, or boats, where it was placed in large steeps, or tanks. Water was then poured over and it was left for around 48 hours to soak thoroughly. It was then spread on the floor of the malting shed with its characteristic Chinese pagoda-like roof ventilators and was left for something like eight days to reach the right stage of germination. To regulate the degree of heat in the malting barley, it was turned at regular intervals. When the required state of germination had been reached, the starch in the barley had all by this time been transformed into sugar. It was then heated in a kiln over peat fires to check the germination, thus imparting a peaty, smoky flavour to the whisky.

Second Stage

The malted grain was then bruised in the mill before being put into the mash tun, where heated water was added and the mixture stirred. The peaty water would add its own flavour and with added yeast the mixture, now known as wort, fermented in special fermenting vats for some three days, during which the sugar was converted into alcohol.

The resulting wash was then led into the wash-still, standing beside the spirit-still.

The Wash-Still and the Spirit-Still

In any malt whisky distillery today, the wash-still and spirit-still may be seen standing side by side, at first sight apparently identical to each other. The wash in the wash-still is heated to the boiling point, when the alcohol rises through the worm, or coil, in its cold-water jacket. It is then discharged as low wines directly into the adjacent spirit-still. The same process of heating the low wines to boiling point then takes place and the same process ensues, but this time the spirit produced is malt whisky. This in turn is placed in oak barrels, preferably casks in which sherry had been kept, and is aged for a minimum of three but generally nearer eight to ten years, or sometimes as much as twelve, fifteen, or more, before becoming accepted as the finest drink that any country could produce.

Unique to Scotland

The process of malt whisky pot-still distillation today is in essentials virtually unchanged from the first quarter of the 19th century. The whiskies themselves, even when produced in almost identical areas, using apparently identical pot-stills and even when using the same water supply, are never the same. Despite all efforts to duplicate the process in other countries, the distilling of Scotch malt whisky remains unique to Scotland.

The Silent Season

During the summer months, when the burns and springs supplying the old distilleries tended to run dry, and when it often grew too warm for the malting process to be carried through successfully, distilling was abandoned for several weeks in what was termed the "silent season." During this period distillery maintenance and repairs were usually carried out. As the autumn set in, distilling would then start again. Some distilleries even today have a silent season when repairs are carried out and distilling is discontinued.

The Introduction of the Continuous Patent-Still

In 1828 a new invention revolutionised the whisky industry when Robert Stein, from one of the Lowland whisky distilling families, produced the first continuous patent-still. This distilled in one continuous process, without the double distillation required in pot-still distillation. Only four years later, in 1832, Aeneas Coffey, an ex-Inspector General of Excise in Ireland, patented a simpler continuous still that became known as the Coffey still and quickly superseded Stein's more cumbersome invention.

The Patent-Still

The continuous still is basically little more than two 40-foot-high copper columns side by side, linked by a junction pipe at the top. These are known as the analyser and rectifier, and each column consists of a number of horizontal compartments containing perforated copper plates. A jet of steam is passed through these columns and the wash is pumped into the still through a pipe coiled around the length of the rectifier from the top downwards, both cooling the latter and also heating the wash before it enters the top of the analyser column. On entering the analyser column, the heated wash encounters an upwards pressure of steam surging through the perforated chambers. Since alcohol boils and evaporates at lower temperatures than water, the alcohol separates from the wash as it descends chamber by chamber through the perforated plates. The alcohol then rises with the steam and, entering the base of the rectifier column, condenses on the perforated plates of each chamber. The purest alcohol rises to the top and the heavier higher alcohols and lower alcohols condense at lower levels since they have lower boiling points and are drawn off for re-distilling. The end product of this method of distilling is almost pure alcohol and since it is a continuous process can be continued as long as wash is available to put through the still.

Grain Whisky

The whisky produced by this process became known as patent-still, or grain, whisky, to differentiate it from the malt whisky produced by the malt whisky distillers, using the slower traditional method requiring two pot-stills. The grain whisky distillers were naturally able to produce far greater quantities of their whisky than the malt whisky distillers and there was keen rivalry between the two, with the slower pot-still distillers inevitably the losers. Since almost all the new patent-stills were situated convenient to the larger centres of population in the Lowlands, there was also an element of the familiar antagonism between Highlander and Lowlander that is even today to be found not far below the surface.

The Merchants

The middle-men who sold the whisky in the mid-19th century, many of whom at this stage were little more than family grocers, began to grow in importance with the growth of the Scotch whisky industry itself. Like middlemen in many other industries, they reaped considerable profits, and their power developed to the stage where they could dictate their own terms to the whisky distillers, more especially the small pot-still malt whisky producers. Being individualists to a man, the latter especially were very slow to combine and while the rest of the Scotch whisky industry gradually began to merge and consolidate, they were the last to see the advantages of union.

Whisky at This Stage

The patent-still, or grain, whisky was made from any grain—oats, rye, or maize—crushed and boiled to break up the starch. During the mashing process a little malted barley would be added; then fermentation on a large scale would take place. The result was that it was not only produced in much larger quantities, but it was much quicker, cheaper, and easier to produce than the slow, twice distilled, pot-still distillation methods. Furthermore, it was generally much more even, being more or less tasteless pure spirit. The malt distillers, seldom operating with more than two or four stills and relying largely on the skill of the individual still-man supervising the distilling process, often produced very varying single malt whiskies (i.e., malt whisky from one distillery unmixed with any other), which not only tasted very strong to southern palates, but also varied considerably with each distilling. To the discerning the differences might be both interesting and desirable, but they did not make it easy to sell. It was only when grain whisky was added to single malt whiskies to make a standardised blend that was smoother and more acceptable to southern palates that sales began to rise.

Blended Whisky

From the 1850s onwards, especially, the growth of the Scotch whisky industry was dramatic. It was a merchant, Andrew Usher & Co., agent for the Glenlivet malt whisky, who is credited with first introducing blended whisky in 1853. The term blended whisky was at first used to describe a mixture of malt whiskies, now known as vatted malts, but in time came to be used to describe the addition of malt whisky to grain whisky, making the blended whiskies we know today. At the time it is doubtful if the full significance of this innovation was appreciated, but inevitably it led to cut-throat competition in the industry as the trade expanded over the second half of the 19th century. By that time, however, the industry had shed its old illicit image and was highly organised with a Customs man then present in each distillery who had charge of a set of keys providing sole access to the spirit-still and bonded store, where the whisky produced was kept to mature.

The Early Cartels

The earliest "trade arrangement," as it was euphemistically termed, was entered into in 1856 by six firms of distillers. In the 1860s the cartel was re-formed and in 1877 the firms concerned decided to merge. They were: John Bald & Co., Carsebridge Distillery, Alloa; John Haig & Co., Cameron Bridge Distillery, Fife; Macfarlane & Co., Port Dundas Distillery, Glasgow; MacNab Bros & Co., Glenochil Distillery, Menstrie; Robert Mowbray, Cambus Distillery, Alloa; Stewart & Co., Kirkliston Distillery, Lothian. Together they formed the Distillers Company Limited, based in Edinburgh, which steadily developed by merger and takeovers to become the leading force in the industry for the best part of a hundred years, attaining its greatest period of strength before and after the 1939–45 War.

The Brand Names

From around 1853 to the 1870s, the blended whiskies sold in the south were often little more than grain whisky with a minimal amount of malt (pot-still) whisky added. Nevertheless, a number of very able, reputable merchants and distillers began to emerge, producing recognised standard whiskies with specific brand names. With consummate salesmanship they spread the sales of Scotch not only throughout England but onto the continent and throughout the British Empire and elsewhere in the civilised world. As a result of their efforts blended whisky came to be recognised throughout the world as the product of Scotland.

Phylloxera Vastatrix and "The Big Five"

The effect of *Phylloxera vastatrix*, a lethal insect that attacked the roots of the vines, on the French wine and, hence, also the brandy, producers had been disastrous in the 1870s and '80s and the producers of Scotch whisky were not long in seizing their opportunity. Scotch whisky soon came to fill the gap in the market. Famous names such as James Buchanan's Black and White, Peter Mackie's White Horse, Alexander Walker's Johnnie Walker, the Dewar brothers, John and Tommy, John Haig, and others had begun to dominate the industry. These, however, were widely known as The Big Five, who were all recognised and celebrated salesmen and founders of famous brand names of various blended whiskies sold widely throughout the world and also widely advertised. The flamboyant salesmanship of Tommy Dewar endeared him to the press and the public, even if it was his brother John who was the steadying influence. James Buchanan's tall, handsome figure and considerable presence made him a powerful personality in any company. Peter Mackie, too, was a man who naturally hit the headlines and influenced the industry. These were amongst the men who dominated the whisky industry during the boom years of the 1880s and '90s. Although the Distillers Company Limited was the growing power behind the scenes, which ultimately under the superb direction of William Ross was to take them all over, they were the names the public chiefly associated with the Scotch whisky industry at this time, and to a large extent they were also responsible for its rapid growth.

Malt Whisky Distillers

This is not to say that the pot-still malt whisky distillers were unable to survive. There were still many small malt whisky distillers and despite the strong and powerful Lowland grain distillers and the power of the merchants they managed to keep going, for there were still considerable local sales within Scotland itself, as well as regular sales to discriminating merchants and blenders who knew what they required. At this stage there were several clear groupings of pot-still malt whisky distillers. There were basically the Highland distillers, notably in Speyside based mainly around the Central Highland Speyside area, and the Lowland distillers below the Highland Line to be found as far south as Dumfriesshire and East Lothian. There were also those on the Islands, mainly on the west coast, particularly on Islay. There were in addition thirty-four concentrated in and around the west coast town of Campbeltown, then known as the malt whisky capital of Scotland. Most of these area groupings, with the notable exception of Campbeltown, remain in existence today.

The End of the Scotch Whisky Boom

Although by the 1890s most of the big brand names we know today such as Black & White, Haig, Queen Anne, Johnnie Walker, and Vat 69, to name only a few, were selling well throughout the world, there were also many dubious fly-by-night firms cashing in on the boom by selling whisky of a very low standard at inflated prices. One of the more flamboyant and dubious firms blending and selling their own whisky at this time were Pattison's Ltd, controlled by two brothers, Robert and Walter Pattison, who had started as dairy wholesalers and graduated to dispensing whisky because they felt there was more profit in that than in selling watered milk. They found they could buy cheap grain whisky at under Is (5p) a gallon and by adding a minute quantity of malt whisky could sell it at 8s 6d (42½p) a gallon, describing it as Finest Glenlivet. One of their more bizarre attempts at advertising included distributing to their retailers some five hundred parrots that were allegedly trained to say "Drink Pattison's Whisky." Despite, or because of, such sales methods they went bankrupt in 1898 to the then almost unheard of sum of £82,000. Investigation soon revealed fraud on a large scale as well as making public the more deplorable methods of blending used by the disreputable end of the whisky industry. Their trial, combined with the outbreak of the Boer War, brought the whisky boom to an abrupt end. It also brought before the public attention for the first time the argument of the pot-still whisky distillers that grain whisky was not really Scotch whisky.

The Islington Borough Council

In 1906 the Islington Borough Council took a local publican to court for selling grain whisky, alleging that this was "not the nature, substance, and quality demanded by the purchaser." The Distillers Company Limited failed to take the case seriously and the result seemed a resounding triumph for the pot-still malt distillers when it was held that "whisky should consist of a spirit distilled in a pot-still derived from malted barley ..."

The Royal Commission of 1909

Although at first hailing this legal decision as a resounding victory, the malt whisky distillers quickly realised that the enormously wealthy Lowland distillers would simply distil very cheap Lowland malts and use them instead of their Highland malts to produce blended whisky. Both sides therefore asked for a Royal Commission to decide the issue and after eighteen months, in 1909, the Commission very sensibly concluded that "whiskey [the current spelling of the period] is a spirit obtained by the distillation of a mash of cereal grains saccharified by the diastase of the malt; that 'Scotch whiskey' is whiskey, as above defined, distilled in Scotland ..." This definition of Scotch whisky was finally incorporated in Statute Law (as late as 1952) and is thus accepted by every government throughout the world. Because of this ruling, Scotch whisky may not be distilled in any other country in the world.

Increasing Taxation

The first increase in taxation for forty years took place in 1900 when it was raised to 11s (55p) from the 10s (50p) per gallon set by Gladstone in 1860. In 1909, taking full advantage of the split in the industry resulting from the Royal Commission's findings, David Lloyd George, then Chancellor of the Exchequer and a lifelong rabid teetotaller, raised the tax per proof gallon by a further 3s 9d

(18½p) to 14s 9d (73½p). Without united opposition from within the industry the increase was passed, a foretaste of things to come and a warning to both distillers and merchants of the dangers of lacking unanimity.

The Scottish Malt Distillers Limited

Just before the outbreak of the 1914–18 War, the Distillers Company Limited, already the most powerful moving force in the industry, amalgamated five Lowland malt whisky distillers into a group called the Scottish Malt Distillers Limited. Inevitably many of the malt whisky distilleries that found themselves unable to survive the rigours of the war years were absorbed into this growing DCL subsidiary.

The Effects of the 1914–18 War

The DCL was large enough to survive the war years and even prosper under the able directorship of its outstanding managing director, William Ross. Its patent-still distilleries were employed in producing industrial alcohol for wartime use. During the entire war the DCL continued to expand, through mergers, amalgamations, and takeovers. In 1917 the government restricted distilling solely to producing industrial alcohol. The Central Liquor Control Board also decreed that all spirits should be diluted to 50 under proof or 70% proof. The industry responded by forming the Whisky Association, a central body to defend the interests of all distillers, both patent-still and pot-still, blenders, merchants, and exporters. In spite of this, the price of whisky rose from 20s to 80s owing to lack of controls.

From 1918 to 1920

In 1918, seeking a means of financing the enormous costs of the war, the government more than doubled the tax per proof gallon of whisky from 14s 9d (73½p) to 30s (£1.50), a total rise of 15s 5d. This naturally produced more revenue in the short term and encouraged the Chancellor of the

Exchequer to add a further 20s (£1) in 1919, making the total tax a matter of 50s (£2.50) per proof gallon, more than trebling the level of taxation within three years. In 1920 the government went even further and raised the tax by 22s 6d (£1.12½) to 72s 6d (£3.62½) per proof gallon, thus making a fivefold increase within three years, the sort of burden that would inevitably be a strain on any industry, not least one attempting to recover from the effects of a major war.

Prohibition

The year 1920 also saw the introduction of Prohibition in the United States of America. Pot-still malt distilling had only been permitted to start again in 1919, with the distillers looking forward to a minor boom in postwar years. The effects of the high taxation and Prohibition caused a major depression in the industry instead, and this lasted throughout the 1920s until the end of Prohibition in 1932, by which time that imprudent if well-intentioned experiment had been totally discredited. During this period of depression in the industry, only the DCL empire was sufficiently strong and powerful to continue to expand. Four of the Big Five, Haig, Johnny Walker, Buchanan, and Dewar, had already been amalgamated, and finally in 1927, but only after his death, Sir Peter Mackie's White Horse Distillers were also absorbed into the DCL. The DCL was by then the only company in the whole industry sufficiently powerful to continue to open up new fields abroad, but even so it was mainly by diversification that it survived successfully, especially after the Great Depression of 1930.

The Pot-Still Malt Distillers Association

In 1926 the Pot-Still Malt Distillers Association of Scotland was formed to replace the old North of Scotland Malt Distillers Association as an all-embracing association of all Scottish malt whisky distillers. It is, however, indicative of how deeply the Depression had affected the industry that in 1933 the association recommended to its members that there should be no distilling at all that year, and by that time there were only fifteen distilleries operating in the whole of Scotland, with several of these only operating on a part-time basis. Although the DCL then controlled thirty-three Highland distilleries in addition to five in Campbeltown and five in Islay, most of these had merely been acquired in order to close them down. Excessive taxation and the closure of the major market of the USA had brought the industry close to total ruin.

The 1930s

From the repeal of Prohibition in 1930 to the outbreak of war in 1939 the industry began to recover. The process started gradually but speeded up as the world markets began slowly to expand. The outbreak of war was not entirely unexpected but was naturally a grave blow, as was the imposition of a further 10s (50p) tax per proof gallon in 1939, raising it to 82s 6d (£4.12½).

The 1939–45 War

In 1940 the duty per proof gallon was raised by 15s (75p) to 97s 6d (£4.87½) and distilling was restricted. It was then prohibited altogether from 1941 to 1945. This did not prevent the tax being raised again in 1942 by a further 40s (£2) to 137s 6d (£6.87½) and yet once more in 1943 by a further 20s (£1) to 157s 6d (£7.87½). From 1945 onwards distilling on a small scale was permitted for pot-still malt whisky distillers only, to earn much-needed dollar currency.

The Scotch Whisky Association

In 1942, recalling their experiences after the 1914–18 War and to provide the industry with the maximum security possible, the Whisky Association was wound up and replaced by the Scotch Whisky Association. Its primary objectives were: to protect and promote the interest of the Scotch whisky trade generally both at home and abroad and to do all things and take all such measures as may be conducive or incidental to the attainment of such objects.

1945–50

Although only very limited pot-still malt distilling had been permitted from 1944 onwards to earn much-needed dollar currency, this did not stop Hugh Dalton, Chancellor of the Exchequer, in 1947 raising the tax per proof gallon by 33s 4d (£1.66½) to 190s 10d (£9.54). In 1948 his successor, Sir Stafford Cripps, added a further 20s (£1) to the tax, making it £10 10s 10d (£10.54) per proof gallon. At the same time only licenses to distil for export were granted, yet inevitably every increase of taxation in Britain was followed by corresponding increases in taxation abroad. It might be said the government cut the throat of their goose while it laid its golden eggs and that many of the ills affecting the industry may be traced back to this period.

The 1950s

Throughout the 1950s the Scotch whisky industry, already greatly weakened by the war years and by excessive taxation, was faced with fresh competition, much of it from North America, in part at least financed by British Government subsidies. It could be claimed this was not only cutting the golden goose's throat, but chopping off its limbs and feeding them to the fox for a short-term financial return.

The 1960s

In spite of repeated warnings of the inevitable effects on the industry, throughout the 1960s successive governments continued the negative policy of raising the tax per proof gallon almost annually. The tax was increased in 1961, 1964, 1965, 1966, and 1968, by which time it had reached £18.85 per proof gallon. The industry sought to protect itself by amalgamations and forming ever larger groups.

The 1970s

During the 1970s, although a similar process continued, there were different forces at work. The British currency was decimalised in 1971. In 1973, with the introduction of Value Added Tax and the entry of Britain into the European Economic Community, the duty on whisky was actually reduced for the first time since 1896. This did not deter successive governments from raising the tax per proof gallon every year from 1973 to 1977. By then the tax per proof gallon amounted to £27.09. This represented duty on a bottle of whisky at the rate of £3.16. Further mergers, amalgamations, and takeovers resulted during this period.

The 1980s

This steady investment of foreign capital into what had always been an intensely Scottish industry continued throughout the 1980s. This was a period of severe recession, but the damage had been done, nor did the process halt. Investment from Japan, the Far East, Europe, Canada, and North America continued, taking full advantage of government subsidies. Once established, such companies have not always acted with the genuine long-term, or even sometimes short-term, interests of the Scotch whisky industry—or for that matter of Scotland, or indeed Britain—at heart. Little else could be expected. To encourage foreign investment to set up in competition and even subsidising them to do so can hardly be desirable and has proved in some cases against the best interests of the industry and of the country. For instance, bulk export of Scotch whisky, especially immature stocks, by such firms has undoubtedly damaged the industry's standing and prestige abroad. This is particularly difficult to control and is merely one of the ways in which the industry has been and may continue to be adversely affected. Along with excessive taxation, this absence of overall control emphasises the lack of understanding of successive governments based in London.

Control of a large part of the industry has also been transferred to London following the 1987 still sub-judice acquisition by Guinness of DCL, later merged with Arthur Bell & Sons and renamed United Distillers plc, and other parts are controlled from North America, Europe, and Japan. This is a serious loss to Scotland and a disastrous situation that has been created by successive governments. It might be argued that it can only finally be cured by governmental action since the Scotch Whisky Association, although a very effective trade association, has no mandate beyond those agreed by its members amongst themselves. By introducing a greater degree of control and passing those powers to a freshly created government-backed body with the interests of the industry and of Scotland at heart, the situation might still be saved. As a first step, for instance, each firm or corporation controlling more than, say, two malt whisky distilleries might by law be forced to base its headquarters in Scotland. The position today is a distorting mirror image of the period in 1823 when government actions had brought about a crisis in the industry, and it is only by radical action such as was taken then that matters can be satisfactorily resolved.

The International Organisation of Legal Metrology

Since 1980 Britain has adopted the standard system of proof measurement of the Common Market, measuring alcohol by percentage of volume at 20°C Sikes 70° equals IOLM 39.9% and 75°= 42.8%: 80°= 45.6%: 100°= 57.1%: 120°= 68.5%: Malt whisky may be purchased at 70°–105° proof measured by Sikes's method. This means they vary from approximately 40% to 60% volume. A proof gallon contains 57.1% alcohol by volume and is 100% proof. 1 gallon = 4.546 litres = 180 fl. oz. 1 gallon = 6 bottles of 26⅔ fl. oz = 75 centilitres or 4 bottles of 40 fl. oz. A proof litre = 100% alcohol by volume and the standard bottle contains 70 cl.

FROM TODAY AND ONWARDS

Now that we are part of the European Economic Community they have decreed that Scotch whisky shall be recognised as Scotch whisky only if it is distilled and produced in Scotland. Furthermore, it must be no less than 40% volume, since at anything less it cannot be checked that it is indeed Scotch whisky. In the coming years the industry may regain the standards that, under foreign ownership or through financial stringency, have sometimes slipped, as when control has been by accountants based overseas interested chiefly in the quickest possible returns on their investments. That is a recipe for disaster that has resulted in bankruptcies in other largely foreign-controlled industries in Scotland and the UK. The industry should also cease to be seduced, as parts of it have been during the past decade or more, by these twin PR weaselwords, marketing and presentation, into change simply for the sake of change, whether it is new bottles, new labels, new colouring, or new advertising. This is an industry where time-tried methods and generations of experience are all-important assets, but, although the distillery's name on the label of a malt whisky is roughly equivalent to *Appelation Controlee* and *premier cru* on a wine bottle, possibly some indication of the standard to be expected might be given beyond those at present customary. For instance, perhaps awards for ageing in the cask for twelve or more years could be introduced corresponding to *Grand Cru,* using the Gaelic adjective Mohr, meaning Great, thus creating *A Malt Whisky Mohr.*

Chapter Two
A General Introduction to Scotch Whisky and to the Directory of Malt Distilleries

A Foreword on Scotch Whisky

It is important to understand something of the background of Scotch whisky making, blending, and the industry as a whole before examining the pot-still malt whiskies in detail. In this brief introduction it is impossible to cover every aspect of the industry, but to appreciate and savour malt whiskies to the full it is necessary to know something of each distillery itself, and these are covered briefly in the pages that follow. Ideally, the distiller himself should supervise each aspect of the operation, from buying the barley direct from the farmer to converting it into malt on the floor of the maltings, seeing that it is carefully turned with wooden rakes on the floor of the maltings and at the right moment dried over peat fires for the mashing and distilling processes. In large, modern distilleries most of these procedures will be automated and the malted barley itself may often be obtained from an outside source, but there are still important individuals in the employ of any pot-still malt distillery on whom a great deal depends.

The Still-Man

One such important employee is the still-man, who is responsible for the actual distilling of the whisky. He decides when to start distilling. Much depends on his judgement of when the foreshots have passed and when the "middle cut" is running. Were he to start too soon or leave matters too late and allow the foreshots and aftershots to mix with the final spirit, the result would not be up to standard. Much depends on him. Even in the best regulated of distilleries, however, it may sometimes happen that some foreshots or aftershots have crept into the distilling. Then it may be that a single bottle in a case has been filled with the last of a cask to the bottom of which the evil-tasting oils have sunk. Although no distiller likes to admit it, such an unpleasant, off-tasting bottle is sometimes found in any distillery's products, the equivalent of a corked bottle of wine, but it is a rare occurrence indeed.

The Master Cooper

The distiller should ideally also have a master cooper to supervise the casks in which the spirit is kept to mature. The wastage from such casks by evaporation can otherwise be considerable and add greatly to his costs. Some degree of evaporation in the cask is anyway inevitable and is known as "the angel's share." The choice of cask is important. American oak is the wood usually preferred. The favoured casks are old oak sherry casks, but many distilleries use reconstructed bourbon casks, which by U.S. law may not be reused. Such casks have proved ideal. As long ago as 1890 the practice of soaking new wooden casks with cheap dark sherry before using them was introduced. Nowadays a compound called pajarate, a sweet colouring mixture made from grape juice and used in Jerez for sherries, is diluted and swilled around new barrels to colour the wood before they are used for whisky. Too much sherry in the whisky can lead to undue sweetness or darker colouring or even undesirable overtones in the whisky, masking the delicate flavours. Too much wood that has not previously been used for maturing sherry, or spirit, may lead to an undesirably woody taste in the whisky stored in them. Either of these may occur if the whisky is too long in the barrel. If the cooper or the still-man is not doing his job efficiently, the distillery can soon go to the wall, and it is a fiercely competitive business.

Modern Technology

Sadly, with the advent of ever more automated systems of distilling, even pot-still distilling is losing the individual touch in many cases. The still-man in places may be seen controlling the whole business in a white coat and watching the dials on a computer. Where there are several stills in one distillery, the likelihood is that the contents of each will be mixed together to make up one standardised single malt whisky rather than allow the individual variations of each distilling to go through to the customer, which used to make pot-still malt whiskies such an exciting business to taste and savour in the same way that each fresh crop of the vineyards produces fresh and exciting vintages. The modern craving for standardisation is a big mistake when applied to malt whiskies.

The Conglomerates

When the big conglomerates take over and try to streamline the industry with numerous stills, vast whisky vats, and control by computer, something inevitably goes out of the product. Sadly, the foreign takeovers of pot-still malt distilleries and the big conglomerate acquisitions have gone almost unopposed because of successive governments' savage taxation of the whisky industry. Fortunately, there are still some shining exceptions.

The Grants

The Grants, particularly, are a resilient clan, to which I am happy to be related, and they have had and continue to have a considerable influence on distilling in Scotland. It is a name that figures largely in any history of pot-still malt whisky distilling. There are, of course, many others who are concerned to see that pot-still distilling of malt whisky should continue in the traditional way to produce fine and distinctive single-malts. This part of the industry is fully alive and continuing to flourish.

BLENDED WHISKY

Blending Scotch whisky is a skilled task accomplished by experts who "nose" their various whiskies, savouring the bouquet and making up the various proportions that form the final blend. As many as thirty, or more, malt whiskies may be used to make up a specific blend. Year after year their task is to produce exactly the same taste in their blend. The major recognised blends do not alter very perceptibly in taste over the years, entirely owing to their expertise. Knowing also the particular tastes of the countries to which their blends are destined for export, they can subtly alter them to match the required demand, not only for taste but also for colour and consistency.

NOSING

Unlike wine, it is not possible simply to taste whisky by swilling the neat spirit around the mouth. To do so would merely be to destroy the sense of taste almost immediately. A single measure of whisky should be poured into a tulip-shaped glass, although a wine glass is satisfactory for most purposes, and at 40% volume a similar quantity of pure water added. If the aroma is then smelt, the expert can deduce the origins of the blend or, if a malt, details of its distilling and maturing process. When the volume is greater he will require to add more pure water accordingly. He will also always start with the less powerful and go on to the stronger, more highly flavoured, since to do otherwise would be to miss the more delicate scents. These, of course, would be lost if chlorinated tap water was used instead of pure water. A heavy smoker, or someone addicted to peppermints or chewing gum, or strong-tasting foods like curries, or anyone with a cold, is unlikely to be able to achieve much by nosing. It is essential to keep the senses of smell and taste as acute as possible, but given practice even a heavy smoker may appreciate something of the differences among malts in this way.

COLOUR

The blender will also bear in mind the colour of whisky preferred by his customer. For instance, the majority of the United States prefers a light-coloured whisky, perhaps on the grounds that a large, light-coloured whisky does not appear any darker in the glass than a small, light-coloured whisky. Since whisky when distilled is almost colourless, some degree of colouring is often added. Although malt whisky may acquire a certain amount of colour while it is being matured in old oak sherry casks, it is an open secret that this can also be due to caramel or even sherry.

Blenders in practice will have a colour chart available to assist them and it is not a difficult matter to produce any colour that is required. So far, thank goodness, no-one has tried to market pink whisky like pink champagne, but no doubt it will not be long before this, too, is tried.

GRAIN WHISKY

Fine Old Cameron Brig produced by Haig at their distillery at Glenrothes in Fife was for a long time the only pure grain whisky for sale. This has now been sold, but others are now available, notably Invergordon. By choosing your own malt whiskies and blending them with these, it is, of course, possible to make your own blended whisky. It is also possible and pleasurable to mix your own malt whiskies to achieve perfection.

DO-IT-YOURSELF

The beauty of Scotch whisky is that it is perfectly possible for the discriminating drinker to make up a blend, or a mixture of malt whiskies, known as a vatted malt whisky, entirely to his own taste, if he wishes to find out whether he can improve on those produced commercially. There is little doubt that by choosing his blends shrewdly and adding a measure of malt whisky to them he can often greatly improve the blend he is drinking, at least to his own satisfaction. The same is undoubtedly true of mixing malt whiskies and producing a vatted malt that is, to his particular taste, an improvement on the originals used to make up the end product. Contrasting malt whiskies by selecting three or four amongst the finest, then, after nosing and savouring them, taking a little of each in differing quantities together in one glass, is always exciting. In this way nectar may be achieved, but in the nature of things it is a nectar that is constantly changing, since the constituents themselves are never quite the same. Over the years, inevitably, malt whiskies change and their characters alter as the men who make them and control their destiny also change.

Drinking Scotch Whisky

How anyone drinks Scotch whisky is entirely up to him. There are cocktails made from Scotch whisky, some of which are even drinkable. Some people prefer to drown the taste of their Scotch whisky in ginger ale, or orange juice. Others always insist on drinking their Scotch, whether malt or blend, neat, on the grounds that it is already watered before sale. Certainly some tap water tastes strongly of chloride and other additives, but to obtain the greatest satisfaction from a mature blend or a fine malt many people will rightly maintain that a little pure water improves the drink, probably as in "nosing" at least an equal quantity of water at 40% volume, but remember, even carbonated spring waters can alter the flavour of a fine malt whisky. It is, however, in the end a matter of individual choice and taste, for Scotch whisky in all its forms is a highly individual drink. It is the product of the country's lochs and rivers, of the barley, the peat, the labour, and the centuries-old expertise of Scots. It is the very essence of Scotland itself. Drink it as you wish, but above all enjoy it.

The Malt Whiskies

There are still over a hundred malt whisky distilleries to be found in Scotland. It is the malt whisky from these that provides the essential flavours of the Scotch itself, whether drunk individually, in conjunction with others as vatted malts, or as blended whisky mixed with grain, or patent-still, whisky. These malt whiskies are to the connoisseur what the *premier cru* wines are to the wine drinker. No two are alike and each separate bottling may differ from the last, although today a high degree of standardisation has been achieved. Whether this is always necessarily a good thing is another matter, but it has to be said that it does make the task of the blender easier. It is, however, still a matter for congratulation that each malt whisky has its own unique taste and aftermath.

Ageing and Maturing

By the legal definition of Scotch whisky contained in the Scotch Whisky Act of 1988, no Scotch whisky may be sold under three years old and most are, in fact, kept in the cask until matured for five years at least. There is usually a particular age at which it is considered that individual malt whiskies achieve their best. This may vary from five to eight years, ten or twelve, or even fifteen and upwards, although in some cases more may be lost than gained after twelve or so. Two or three years, then, may make a big difference. Some malt whiskies mature faster than others. Where no age is given for a malt whisky it is reasonable to assume around five, or at most six. Lowland malt whiskies are generally said to be mature enough to bottle at five years. It should be added that while whisky matures and alters perceptibly while kept in a cask, it is unlike wine in that it does not alter materially once bottled.

The Geography of Malt Whisky

The malt whiskies are widely separated geographically but there are basically only two main divisions, Highland and Lowland, from above and below the Highland Line. There are, however, quite a number of west coast Highland and northern Highland malt whiskies as well as a large grouping around Speyside. There are also Island malt whiskies, particularly the Islay group and those from Orkney. Fortunately, the products of the different regions as well as of the individual distilleries remain each as different from the next as claret from burgundy or sherry from port. It is this that makes the malt whiskies so satisfying to savour even if there may be general similarities of type amongst the various groups. The large grouping around Speyside may have certain recognisable similarities, but they also differ widely from each other and from other Highland groups. The Islay malt whiskies also have their own very recognisable characteristics, but again differ very much from each other. The two remaining Campbeltown malt whiskies still have a distinctive flavour of their own, as do those of Orkney, Highland Park, and Scapa. So it is with the Lowland malt whiskies. There is a wealth of choice for the enthusiast.

The Single Scotch Malt Whisky

A Question of Definition

If you wish to be exact, it is correct to refer to the product of a single pot-still malt whisky distillery in Scotland as a single Scotch malt whisky. The reason for calling it Scotch malt whisky is that, although not many people are likely to encounter their products in this country, there is a pot-still malt whisky distillery in Ireland and three or four in Japan, notably Suntory's, started in 1923. The reason for terming it single is that even if what is in the cask is the result of several distillations, it is the product of a single distillery as distinct from a vatted malt whisky, which is the product of several distilleries. This is, however, really being pedantic and leads to the absurdity that if you then wish to refer to the product of one distillation that has been casked as such it has to be termed a "single-single malt." The answer is always to refer to vatted malts as vatted malts and to refer to single Scotch malt whisky simply as malt whisky.

The Labelling

The label on malt whisky bottles, like the shape of the bottles themselves, is liable to change from time to time, but there are certain points that should remain constant. It should specify that it is a product of Scotland, and that it is a pure malt whisky, giving the area from which it is produced and the name of the distillery and the name of the malt whisky itself, if different, as a few are. The alcoholic strength at which it is sold must be noted, as must the quantity in the bottle. The age should also be given, although some malt whiskies are sold with the age unspecified. If it is bottled by an independent bottler this will be specified, in which case it must be appreciated that it cannot be regarded as a true sample of the distillery's product since such bottlings are liable to alter from year to year in strength and in age. To give the year of the bottling, as with a wine, means nothing since whisky once in a bottle does not alter materially. If it is a blended whisky, it should specify that it is Scotch whisky and a product of Scotland. It should also add "distilled, blended, and bottled in Scotland." If it is a vatted malt, probably styled *The Pride of this and that,* it may say that it is "pure malt" and it may give an age, which, as is the case with blended whisky, must be the age of the youngest constituent, but it will not include the name of a distillery. There should be no confusion and it is simply a question of reading the label of the bottle with care. The same applies to the very numerous blended whiskies that must of necessity be left outside the scope of this book, although a listing of some of the better-known vatted malts has been included. (See pages 152–156.)

A Question of Taste

In describing taste, which is such an individual matter, it is next to impossible to be exact, and what one man likes another may abhor. It may be said that every Scot is basically an east coast man or a west coast man, depending on which side of Scotland he was born. To the east coast man initially the west coast malts taste of seaweed and drains. To the west coast man the east coast malts taste of antiseptic. It is only by persevering that the east coast man will discover subtle differing flavours and the west coast man surprising delicate nuances of taste. I have tried to avoid generalities or vague descriptions such as nutty, which may be coconut or hazelnut or peanut or whatever, but describing what amounts to mere sensations is at times a near impossibility. Poetic flights of fancy suggesting, for instance, a peppermint flavour to a whisky are to my mind unhelpful and downright impossible unless it is adulterated. As far as possible I have tried to indicate the taste as plainly as possible, but it is up to everyone to make up his own mind; that is half the pleasure of the drink.

A Question of Time and Place

The short answer as to when it is best to drink Scotch whisky is any time you feel like it. In practice many outside factors must influence the matter. Extremes of temperature, whether of heat or cold, are one obvious factor. The state of mind and body is another. Clearly a dram is likely to be savoured with more appreciation after a day in the open air rather than in the smoky atmosphere of a city when no exercise has been taken. Scotch whisky can best be savoured in Scotland itself where it was distilled, but it travels well around the world and provides a taste of Scotland anywhere at any time. In the subsequent pages I have indicated that some malt whiskies may perhaps best be savoured before and some after a meal, but this is purely a pointer and not in any sense a firm guide. Everyone should make his own decision on this score.

INDEPENDENT BOTTLING

There is nothing to stop anyone from buying malt whisky in the cask and storing it to have it bottled for himself when he wishes. In practice it is a very sensible way of buying malt whisky, and various societies and syndicates with a special interest in malt whisky do so. Two independent bottlers in particular are also well known for the practice. These are Gordon & MacPhail Ltd, 58-60 South St, Elgin, Morayshire, IV30 IYJ, and William Cadenhead Ltd, 172 Canongate, Edinburgh, EH8 8BN. Anyone interested in malt whisky owes a debt to these firms for providing many single-malts that would otherwise be unobtainable. The Scotch Malt Whisky Society, situated at The Vaults, Leith, 87 Giles St, Edinburgh, EH6 6BZ, performs a like service for some 16,000 members. On the other hand, since these bottlings vary considerably in age and strength, it is unfair and unreasonable to attempt to describe a distillery's malt whisky from them. They are like an old, long-bottled vintage port, delightful and rewarding, but unrepeatable and not representative of modern standard bottlings.

PUBLICITY REGARDING DISTILLERIES

The Scotch Whisky Heritage Centre, 358 Castlehill, Edinburgh, open seven days a week (tel: 0131 220 0441), by the Castle entrance, is fun and informative for visitors of any age and sex, from family parties to organised groups. Here you may learn painlessly all the facts about distilling and you can ride in half a whisky barrel for an audiovisual journey through the centuries, giving all the information on Scotch whisky anyone could want in six languages. Whisky tastings are also arranged. The Cairngorm Whisky Centre and Museum at Aviemore is also worth visiting, as is the old distillery at Dallas Dhu near Forres. (See p. 154.) The Scottish Tourist Board at Ravelston Crescent, Edinburgh (tel: 0131 332 2433) and local tourist offices in the Grampian and Highland Regions will also give details of those distilleries open for visitors, or on The Whisky Trail. Even where they have reception centres, however, their main task is distilling whisky, so it is advisable to telephone beforehand.

Particulars of Distilleries

It is important to know where each distillery is, a little of its background history, so that one can judge how much continuity and experience lie behind it, also who exactly owns it and to whom it is licensed, both very pertinent points. If you happen to be in the area, it is as well to know whether you can visit it and whether it is accustomed to dealing with visitors. Finally, some idea of what the product tastes like cannot come amiss. From the particulars of the distilleries that follow in alphabetical order, the reader should learn quite a lot about the making of malt whisky and the development of the industry itself.

The Individual Choice

Since all taste is a matter for the individual to make up his or her own mind about, it is impossible to do more than make suggestions and point the individual in the right direction. The basic information is here. It is up to each reader to go on as far as he wishes in his or her own way. It has often been argued that there is no such thing as bad Scotch whisky and it is up to everyone to make his or her own choice. There is certainly a great deal of satisfaction to be had from any Scotch whisky distilled in Scotland, but in the ensuing pages we are concerned with the original Scotch whisky that was distilled before the invention of the patent-still. In discovering the infinite variety and satisfaction to be had from the malt whiskies, distilled in the pot-stills of Scotland, the reader who has never sampled them before should find great enjoyment. Even those who have already grown to know and savour the flavours of the various malt whiskies may learn something from what follows. *Slainte!*

Distillery Groupings

(*signifies generally available; nc, not commercially available; m, mothballed and not currently operational; c, closed)

Allied Distillers Ltd Ardbeg (Islay m nc), Ardmore (Speyside nc), *Balblair (Highland Northern), *Glenburgie (Speyside), Glencadam (Highland Eastern nc), *Glendronach (Speyside), *Glentauchers (Speyside), Imperial (Speyside nc), Inverleven (Lowland Northern c), *Laphroaig (Islay), Lomond (Lowland Northern c), *Miltonduff (Speyside), *Tormore (Speyside), Scapa (Orkney nc).

Burn Stewart Distillers plc* Deanston (Highland Southern), *Tobermory (Island, Mull)

Destilerias y Crianza del Whisky, Madrid *Lochside (Highland Eastern c)

General Beverage Corpn., Luxembourg Macduff (*Glen Deveron: Speyside)

J & G Grant *Glenfarclas (Speyside)

Wm Grant & Son *Balvenie (Speyside), Kininvie (Speyside nc), *Glenfiddich (Speyside) (Grain: Ladyburn, Girvan)

Highland Distilleries Co plc *Bunnahabhain (Islay), Glenglassaugh (Speyside c), *Glenrothes (Speyside), *Glenturret (Highland South), *Highland Park (Orkney), *Tamdhu (Speyside)

International Distillers Vintners *Auchroisk (The Singleton Speyside), *Glen Spey (Speyside), *Knockando (Speyside), Strathmill (Speyside nc)

Inver House Distillers Knockdhu (*An Cnoc, Speyside), *Speyburn (Speyside), Pulteney (*Old Pulteney Highland Northern)

Lang Brothers (Robertson & Baxter) *Glengoyne (Highland South West)

Loch Lomond Distillery Co. Ltd. *Glen Scotia (Campbeltown), Littlemill (Lowland West c), Loch Lomond (*Inchmurrin, *Rossdhu, Highland Southwest) (Grain: Loch Lomond)

Macallan Distillers *Macallan (Speyside)

Macdonald Martin Distilleries *Glen Moray (Speyside), *Glenmorangie (Highland Northern)

J & A Mitchell *Springbank (*Longrow Campbeltown)

Morrison Bowmore *Auchentoshan (Lowland), *Bowmore (Islay), *Glen Garioch (Highland East)

Nikka Ben Nevis (Highland Western nc)

Ricard International *Aberlour (Speyside), *Edradour (Highland Southern), *Glenallachie (Speyside)

Seagram Allt-a-Bhainne (Speyside nc), *Benriach (Highland), Braeval (Speyside nc), Caperdonich (Speyside), *The Glenlivet (Speyside), *Glen Grant (Speyside), *Glen Keith (Speyside), *Longmorn (Speyside), *Strathisla (Speyside)

Speyside Distillery Co. Ltd Speyside (*Drumguish, Speyside)

Takara Shuzo & Okura *Tomatin (Highland Eastern)

United Distillers plc *Aberfeldy (Highland), *Aultmore (Speyside), Balmenach (Speyside m nc), *Benrinnes (Speyside), *Blair Athol (Highland), *Cragganmore (Speyside), *Craigellachie (Speyside), *Caol Isla (Islay), Cardhu (Speyside),*Clynelish (Highland Northern), Coleburn (Speyside c), *Dailuaine (Speyside), *Dalwhinnie (Highland Central), *Dufftown-Glenlivet (Speyside), *Glen Elgin (Speyside), Glen Esk (Highland Eastern c nc), *Glen Ord (Highland Northern), *Glendullan (Speyside), *Glenkinchie (Lowland), *Glenlossie (Speyside), *Inchgower (Speyside), Lagavulin (Islay), *Linkwood (Speyside), *Mannochmore (Speyside), *Mortlach (Speyside), *Oban (Highland Western), Pittyvaich (Speyside c nc), *Royal Brackla (Highland North-ern), *Royal Lochnagar (Speyside), *Teaninich (Highland Northern), *Talisker (Island, Skye)

Whyte & Mackay Bruichladdich (Islay m), *Dalmore (Highland Northern), *Fettercairn (Highland East), *Isle of Jura (Island, Jura), Tamnavulin-Glenlivet (Speyside m), *Tomintoul-Glenlivet (Speyside), Tullibardine (Highland Southern m) (Grain: *Invergordon)

Aberfeldy

Situation

Aberfeldy, Perthshire. 32 miles northwest of Perth. Tayside Region

Classification

Highland (Southern)

Origins and Background

Built by the Dewar brothers, John and Tommy, in the 1890s near where their father had been born. It may possibly have been intended as a memorial to him, but it was more probably seen as a seal on his and their success story, from crofters to distilling magnates in two generations. On their merger with the DCL in 1925 it became a part of the DCL empire, now themselves merged into United Distillers plc.

Owned By

United Distillers plc

VISITORS

Reception Centre. Tel: 01887 820330

AGE AND STRENGTH WHEN BOTTLED

10 years at 40% volume and 15 years at 43% volume

COMMENTS

Most still goes for blending, presumably for John Dewar's blends, but United Distillers have wisely changed DCL's policy and are now making at least limited stocks of most single malts available at the distilleries and selected outlets. This is a clean, light-bodied, highland single malt that makes a good dram that merits wider marketing.

ABERLOUR

SITUATION

Near Ben Rinnes southwest of Keith, in the Spey Valley. Grampian Region

CLASSIFICATION

Highland (Speyside)

ORIGINS AND BACKGROUND

A distillery was first built here in 1826 by James Gordon. Subsequently, a second distillery was built on the site in 1879 by a local banker, James Fleming. It was severely damaged by fire and was sold in 1892 to R. Thorne and Sons Ltd. They rebuilt and expanded it. It was bought by S. Campbell & Son Ltd in 1945 but in 1974 they were taken over by Pernod Ricard, now part of Ricard International SA. Like so many Speyside distilleries, it is delightfully positioned close to the Spey and well screened from the road by a pine wood. Its water comes from the Well of Drostan, which has connections with St Dunstan and Glastonbury. The present distillery has been comprehensively modernised and, as might be expected, the malt whisky it produces has been widely sold in France.

OWNED BY

Ricard International SA

VISITORS

Reception Centre. Tel: 01340 871204

AGE AND STRENGTH WHEN BOTTLED

12 years at 43% volume

COMMENTS

This is a very good, clean postprandial dram, full bodied and smooth with no need to cling to the Glenlivet affix, which has led to this being termed the longest Glen in Scotland.

ALLT-A-BHAINNE *(alt-a-bane)*

SITUATION

4 miles southwest of Dufftown on the slopes of Ben Rinnes. Grampian Region

CLASSIFICATION

Highland (Speyside)

ORIGINS AND BACKGROUND

The name Allt-a-Bhainne means in Gaelic "the milk burn," signifying in this case perhaps a smooth malt whisky. Opened in 1975 by Seagrams at a cost of £2.7 million, this distillery uses the most modern equipment and is very carefully landscaped to fit in with the surrounding countryside. Its capacity of about 1 million proof gallons, or 2.595 million litres of alcohol, was doubled in 1989. This is one of the latest distilleries to open in the region. Unfortunately, it is not sold as a single malt.

OWNED BY

Seagram Distillers plc

VISITORS

By arrangement

AGE AND STRENGTH WHEN BOTTLED

Only bottled by the independent bottlers

COMMENTS

It seems a smooth, clean dram, but it is difficult to judge when only tasted in a 100% proof independent bottling.

ARDBEG

SITUATION
Port Ellen, Islay, Argyll. Strathclyde Region

CLASSIFICATION
Islay

ORIGINS AND BACKGROUND
Established by the McDougall family around 1815 on a site used originally for illicit distilling, this distillery remained privately owned until taken over by Hiram Walker in 1979. The water is obtained from two lochs inland from the distillery, Loch Arinambeast and Loch Uigeadale. The local barley and local peat are also used and production is only around 300,000 proof gallons a year, or 778,500 litres of alcohol, mostly used in blending. The distillery was closed, but reopened in 1989. Now mothballed.

OWNED BY
Allied Distillers Ltd

VISITORS
No

AGE AND STRENGTH WHEN BOTTLED
10 years at 40% volume

COMMENTS
This is a distinctively Islay malt whisky, unmistakably west coast. It has a full body and also a distinctive iodine aftermath. It is definitely an after-dinner drink, and it is hoped that the distillery will soon reopen.

ARDMORE

SITUATION

At Kennethmont, 17 miles south of Huntly. Grampian Region

CLASSIFICATION

Highland (Speyside)

ORIGINS AND BACKGROUND

Built by William Teacher's sons in 1891 when they realised the importance of having their own direct access to supplies of malt whisky for blending purposes. It was modernised and greatly enlarged in the 1950s, when William Teacher remained one of the largest independent whisky distillers still in the control of the original family. They were taken over by Allied Breweries in 1976 and are now part of Allied Distillers Ltd.

OWNED BY

Allied Distillers Ltd

VISITORS

By arrangement

AGE AND STRENGTH WHEN BOTTLED

Only bottled by independent bottlers

COMMENTS

This has always been retained by William Teacher and Sons as the basis for their famous blend and as such only a little has found its way onto the market through the independent bottlers. From a sample bottled by Wm Cadenhead at 18 years and 46% volume, it appears to be a reasonable after-dinner dram with a pleasing aroma and aftermath. It should merit bottling.

AUCHENTOSHAN

SITUATION

Ten miles north of Glasgow at Duntocher, Dunbartonshire.
Strathclyde Region

CLASSIFICATION

Lowland

ORIGINS AND BACKGROUND

Established in 1825 on the road from Glasgow to Dumbarton, it was badly damaged by bombs during the 1939–45 War but was completely rebuilt and modernised. Acquired in 1984 by Stanley P. Morrison Ltd, still a private company, but now Morrison Bowmore Distillers Ltd. (See Bowmore and Glen Garioch.) It lies just below the Highland Line so the whisky is technically a Lowland malt although peat and water are obtained from north of the Line. The latter is from Loch Cochno in the Kilpatrick Hills. The distilling process is unusual in that three stills are used instead of the customary two. The whisky is therefore triple-distilled and possibly this may be responsible for producing a lighter malt than usual.

OWNED BY

Morrison Bowmore Distillers Ltd

VISITORS

Reception centre. Tel: 01389 876561

AGE AND STRENGTH WHEN BOTTLED

10 years at 40% and 21 years at 43% volume

COMMENTS

Perhaps because of its special triple distillation it is a very light and clean-tasting dram at 10 years, but not surprisingly much superior at 21 years, with more body than might be expected.

Auchroisk

Situation

Mulben, Banffshire. Grampian Region

Classification

Highland (Speyside)

Origins and Background

Auchroisk is somewhat unusual, being newly built in 1974 by the International Distillers and Vintners Ltd, and taking its name from a nearby farm, the Gaelic meaning of which is "the ford over the red stream." The water for the distillery is drawn from a spring known as Dorie's Well, which provides an ample supply. As might be expected, the buildings are extremely modern but blend well with the countryside. This amounted to a multimillion pound investment and the eight stills have a production capacity of 1.6 million gallons, or 7.3 million litres of alcohol. The malt whisky is marketed under the name The Singleton on the pretext that Auchroisk is not easily pronounced.

Owned By

International Distillers and Vintners Ltd

Visitors

By arrangement only. Tel: 01542 860333

Age and Strength When Bottled

10 years old at 40% and 43% volume

Comments

Although a modern distillery, the malt whisky produced is a pleasing, smooth after-dinner dram with a good aftermath. Clearly a lot must go for blending, but it is readily available.

Aultmore

Situation

About 3 miles from Keith and 9 miles from Buckie. Grampian Region

Classification

Highland (Speyside)

Origins and Background

The distillery was originally built in 1896 by Alexander Edward of Sanquhar. In 1899 as managing director of a company with the resounding title of The Oban and Aultmore Glenlivet Distillery Co. Ltd, Alexander Edward relinquished ownership to the newly formed company, which controlled both distilleries. In the hard times of 1923 Aultmore was acquired by John Dewar & Sons Ltd, thus becoming part of the DCL and hence now part of United Distillers plc under overall control of Guinness plc.

Owned By

United Distillers plc

Visitors

No

Age and Strength When Bottled

12 years old at 43% volume

Comments

At one time apparently regarded as being in "the longest glen in Scotland," it no longer flaunts the misleading Glenlivet affix and has no need to do so. Although quite a lot must go for blending, this malt whisky is readily available and makes a very good after-dinner drink. It is a good, smooth dram with a clean, dry aftermath.

BALBLAIR

SITUATION
Edderton, near Tain, Ross-shire. Highland Region

CLASSIFICATION
Highland (Northern)

ORIGINS AND BACKGROUND
Dating back to 1790, or possibly even earlier to around 1750, this distillery may claim to be amongst the oldest in Scotland. The distillery on the present site, however, dates from 1872, when it was very greatly developed by Andrew Ross & Son, the owners at that time. Edderton is well supplied with both ample peat and water, which is of course a considerable asset to the distillery. It was acquired by Hiram Walker in 1969. It is considered a fast-maturing malt whisky.

OWNED BY
Allied Distillers Ltd

VISITORS
Reception Centre. Tel: 01862 821273

AGE AND STRENGTH WHEN BOTTLED
5 years at 40% volume

COMMENTS
Most of this malt whisky goes for blending, but some is bottled, mainly for export, and some is bottled by the independent bottlers Gordon & MacPhail. At 5 years, possibly a trifle young, but a pleasing light and rather dry dram with clean aftermath, which is much appreciated by the Italians.

BALMENACH

SITUATION

Balmenach, Cromdale, Grantown-on-Spey, Morayshire. Grampian Region

CLASSIFICATION

Highland (Speyside)

ORIGINS AND BACKGROUND

The original founder was one James MacGregor, who was undoubtedly an illicit distiller when he started in 1801, but he took out a license in 1824 and the distillery officially dates from then. As well as founding the distillery and running it for many years, James MacGregor was the grandfather of Robert Bruce Lockhart, who describes it delightfully in his book, *Scotch.* In the same great storm of 28th December 1879 that caused the Tay Bridge disaster, the distillery chimney stack collapsed and there was nearly a fire, but the situation was saved by the still-man, who opened the discharge cocks and allowed the spirit to run out, thus preventing the fire spreading. In 1897 the grandson of the founder formed the Balmenach-Glenlivet Distillery Ltd, thus adding the affix Glenlivet to the product. In 1922, during the lean postwar years, control passed to DCL, hence to United Distillers plc. Closed in 1993.

OWNED BY

United Distillers plc

VISITORS

No

AGE AND STRENGTH WHEN BOTTLED

12 years at 43% volume

COMMENTS

Unfortunately, this is now really only available through the independent bottlers and it is therefore unfair to make comparisons. From various tastings, however, it seems to be an interesting after-dinner dram, and it is hoped that it will become available again.

BALVENIE

SITUATION
Dufftown, Banffshire. Grampian Region

CLASSIFICATION
Highland (Speyside)

ORIGINS AND BACKGROUND
Dufftown is now rated as Scotland's whisky capital since the eclipse of Campbeltown. A local jingle runs:

Rome was built on seven hills
Dufftown stands on seven stills.

The distillery was established in 1890 by William Grant on part of the land he had bought for his nearby Glenfiddich distillery. The water for distilling is obtained from the fine Robbie Dubh spring and both distilleries use the nearby Fiddich Burn for cooling purposes. Still owned by the firm of William Grant & Sons Ltd, the distillery was greatly expanded in 1955. Balvenie now has its own maltings and supplies malt for Glenfiddich, which has its own bottling plant and in return bottles for Balvenie.

OWNED BY
William Grant & Sons Ltd

VISITORS
Mornings only, by arrangement

AGE AND STRENGTH WHEN BOTTLED
No age given at 40% and 43% volume

COMMENTS
The Balvenie Founders reserve at 40% volume is a vatting of distillates from casks of between 10 and 12 years. It has an initially sweet approach and very satisfying aftermath. The Balvenie Classic at 43% volume is vatted from casks at least 12 years old and is, not surprisingly, a little richer and more mellow with an even longer aftermath. Both are very good drams, but with no resemblance to nearby Glenfiddich.

BEN NEVIS

SITUATION
Ben Nevis, Fort William, Inverness-shire. Highland Region

CLASSIFICATION
Highland (Western)

ORIGINS AND BACKGROUND
Built in 1825 by "Long John" Macdonald, a local farmer turned distiller who claimed descent from the Lords of the Isles and was noted for his outstanding physique as well as the fact that he stood the remarkable height of 6 feet 4 inches. He presented Queen Victoria with a cask of Ben Nevis malt whisky on her visit to Fort William in 1848 and on his death in 1856 was succeeded by his son Donald, followed in turn by his son John. In 1941 the Ben Nevis Distillers (Fort William) Ltd was acquired by the owner of the Great Glen, Joseph Hobbs, who added a grain still, but in 1978 the distillery closed. In 1981 it was bought by Long John International Ltd, a subsidiary of Seager Evans and Whitbread & Co, Ltd. In 1984 distilling restarted, but ceased again in 1986. In 1989, however, it was acquired by the Nikka Whisky Distilling Co., Ltd, of Japan and distilling started once again in 1990.

OWNED BY
Nikka Whisky Distilling Co.

VISITORS
Reception centre. Tel: 01397 700200

AGE AND STRENGTH WHEN BOTTLED
Ad hoc bottlings; e.g., at 19 years and 46% volume

COMMENTS
Since 1978 there has been no chance for a steady programme of distilling. In a few years time it may be bottled regularly again and from the samples available should be worth the wait.

BENRIACH

SITUATION

Next to Longmorn just south of Elgin, Morayshire. Grampian Region

CLASSIFICATION

Highland

ORIGINS AND BACKGROUND

Built by John Duff in the whisky boom of the 1890s next to the Longmorn distillery. It has plentiful supplies of local spring water and peat from Mannoch Hill. It was closed from 1903 to 1965, but has been producing a very good whisky since then, although only bottled by the independent bottlers.

OWNED BY

Seagram Distillers plc

VISITORS

By arrangement

AGE AND STRENGTH WHEN BOTTLED

10 years and 43% volume

COMMENTS

Although close to Longmorn, very different, but still light and extremely delicate. A large proportion still goes for blending, but it is now bottled and sold at 10 years old. A good preprandial dram.

BENRINNES

SITUATION
Benrinnes, Aberlour, Banffshire. Grampian Region

CLASSIFICATION
Highland (Speyside)

ORIGINS AND BACKGROUND
Naturally the distillery is named after nearby Ben Rinnes, from which it obtains its water supplies. It was built in 1897 towards the very end of the Scotch whisky boom and operated successfully and independently until the lean years after the First World War. It was then acquired by John Dewar & Sons Ltd, who took it over under their name in 1926. With their takeover by DCL it was transferred to the Scottish Malt Distillers Ltd, and passed to the present License holders. It has continued operating since then except for very brief closures at the start of the 1930s and in 1943 during the last war.

OWNED BY
United Distillers plc

VISITORS
No

AGE AND STRENGTH WHEN BOTTLED
15 years at 43% volume

COMMENTS
Previously obtainable only through the independent bottlers, but owing to United Distillers' welcome change of policy, it is now available from the distillery and selected outlets and makes a very pleasing aperitif with a delicate, dry, peaty aftermath.

Bladnoch

Situation

1 mile southeast of Wigtown. Dumfries & Galloway Region

Classification

Lowland (Southwestern)

Origins

This most southerly of all the Scottish malt distilleries was founded in 1817 by the McClelland family at the lower end of the village of Bladnoch, from which it takes its name. It has had a somewhat varied history with three distinct periods of expansion followed by temporary closures. After changing hands a number of times, it was finally closed for 18 years from the start of the 1939–45 war years, during which period it even had the stills removed and sent to Sweden. It was only reopened in 1956, changing hands several more times until bought by Arthur Bell & Sons in 1983 from Inver House Distillers Ltd, hence then controlled by United Distillers plc. In 1994 it was sold and distilling ended, but it may remain open as a Heritage Centre.

Owned by

Coordinated Developments

Visitors

Undetermined as yet

Age and strength when bottled

10 years at 43% volume

Comments

This Lowland malt whisky is a very pleasing smooth dram with a light, clean flavour and surprising aftermath. It is a great shame that this, the southernmost distillery in Scotland, is no longer operative and that by the year 2000 this dram will be little more than a memory.

Blair Athol

Situation

Blair Athol, Pitlochry, Perthshire. Tayside Region

Classification

Highland (Central)

Origins and Background

Said to have been founded in 1825, this distillery obtains its water from the Kinnaird Burn and the mountain springs of Ben Vrackie above Pitlochry. Although misleadingly named after the village close to the ducal seat at Blair Castle, it has an attractive position in this well-known tourist centre. It was initially run by Alexander Connacher & Co., but was acquired by P. Mackenzie & Co., Distillers Ltd, of Edinburgh, who greatly enlarged it. After the lean 1914–18 war years it was closed until bought by Arthur Bell & Sons Ltd in 1949, when it was rebuilt. In 1973 the number of stills was doubled from two to four. Since 1988 it has been controlled by United Distillers plc.

Owned By

United Distillers plc

Visitors

Reception Centre. Tel: 01796 472234

Age and Strength When Bottled

12 years at 43% volume

Comments

A lot of this is no doubt used for blending by Arthur Bell & Sons, but it is readily available as a malt whisky. It is an interesting full-bodied dry dram with very little aftermath that makes a good drink before a meal.

BOWMORE

SITUATION

Isle of Islay, on the shore of Loch Indaal and actually right on the sea

CLASSIFICATION

West Coast Islay

ORIGINS AND BACKGROUND

Bowmore was founded in 1779 by a Mr Simson and is the second oldest distillery on Islay. It was expanded by a James Mutter in the late 19th century until the 1890s, when it was taken over by the Bowmore Distillery Co. Ltd. It has now been acquired by the Morrison Bowmore Distillers Ltd.

OWNED BY

Morrison Bowmore Distillers Ltd.

VISITORS

Reception centre. Tel: 01496 810441

AGE AND STRENGTH WHEN BOTTLED

Legend at 40% volume and 12, 17, 21 and 25 years at 43% volume

COMMENTS

A smooth and pleasing after-dinner Islay malt whisky, without quite as much of the heaviness characteristic of many of the Islay malts and with a distinct character of its own.

BRACKLA: *see* ROYAL BRACKLA

BRAEVAL

SITUATION

9 miles southwest of Dufftown, The Braes of Glenlivet. Grampian Region

CLASSIFICATION

Highland (Speyside)

ORIGINS AND BACKGROUND

Opened in 1973 by Seagram Distillers plc named Braes of Glenlivet, when they still had not taken over The Glenlivet Distillers. Hence the reason at the time of building this distillery for the addition of the Glenlivet affix to the name, although it does, in fact, have more reason for the addition than many others, being closer to the Glenlivet distillery than any other. Although the design of the distillery is fairly traditional, it naturally employs all the latest engineering and production techniques. It has a capacity of over a million proof gallons a year or 2.595 million litres of alcohol. Two wells close to the distillery, the Preenie and Kate's Well, provide the water supply for the distilling process. The name was changed in 1994 to Braeval, the name of the croft on which the distillery was built.

OWNED BY

Seagram Distillers plc

VISITORS

By arrangement

AGE AND STRENGTH WHEN BOTTLED

All is used for blending, but some is sometimes bottled by the independent bottlers

COMMENTS

This should be a very interesting malt whisky if any was freed for consumption by the public, and with the change of name a change of policy may follow.

BRORA: *see* CLYNELISH

BRUICHLADDICH *(brew-ich-lad-die)*

SITUATION

Bruichladdich, Isle of Islay, Argyll. Strathclyde Region

CLASSIFICATION

Islay

ORIGINS AND BACKGROUND

This is another Islay distillery right on the sea. It was built in 1881 by the Harvey family, well-known distillers, who formed John and Robert Harvey Limited. From 1886 onwards they ran their Islay distillery as the Bruichladdich Distillery Co. (Islay) Ltd, and it continued thus until its closure in 1938 and acquisition ultimately by the National Distillers of America, who controlled it through a holding company, Train & McIntyre, who incorporated it into their distilling side, Associated Scottish Distillers. After further changes of ownership the distillery was acquired by Invergordon Distillers Ltd in 1968, who added two new stills and general expansion so that it now has a capacity of 800,000 proof gallons or 2,076,000 litres of alcohol. Its water supplies are obtained from an inland reservoir. It was acquired by Whyte & Mackay in 1993 and mothballed in 1995.

OWNED BY

Whyte & Mackay Distillers Ltd

VISITORS

No

AGE AND STRENGTH WHEN BOTTLED

10, 15, and 21 years at 40% volume

COMMENTS

Perhaps because its water supply comes from inland, this is not like many other Islay malt whiskies. It is a very good aperitif, light and peaty, and although a very pleasing dram, it is not as heavy as others on Islay.

BUNNAHABHAIN *(bun-a-hav-an)*

SITUATION

Bunnahabhain, Port Askaig, Islay, Argyll. Strathclyde Region

CLASSIFICATION

Islay

ORIGINS AND BACKGROUND

Built on the northeast coast of Islay, Bunnahabhain started distilling in 1883. The Islay Distillery Co., which controlled the distillery, merged in 1887 to become part of the Highland Distilleries Company plc, which controls the notable blend The Famous Grouse, taken over in 1970 along with Matthew Gloag & Son Ltd. Since that date the group has expanded remarkably. Until recently almost all the product of the distillery was utilised for blending.

OWNED BY

Highland Distilleries Co. plc

VISITORS

Reception Centre. Tel: 01496 840646

AGE AND STRENGTH WHEN BOTTLED

12 years at 40% volume

COMMENTS

A good after-dinner dram, but not obviously an Islay malt whisky, although with a full-bodied flavour it leaves a good aftermath.

CAOL ILA *(coal-eela)*

SITUATION
Caol Ila, Port Askaig, Islay, Argyll. Strathclyde Region

CLASSIFICATION
Islay

ORIGINS AND BACKGROUND
Possibly founded around 1846, Caol Ila is situated in the most sheltered bay on Islay north of Port Askaig and overlooking the Sound of Jura. It has its own private wharf through which it obtains its own barley and ships off its whisky in return. It gets its water supplies from Loch Torrabus, said to be the finest on Islay. The owners from 1880 to 1920 were Bulloch Lade & Co. Ltd, who were a subsidiary of Robertson & Baxter Ltd. In 1920 they formed Caol Ila Distillery Co. Ltd to run the distillery. When DCL took them over in 1927, the management reverted to Bulloch Lade & Co. Ltd. Only a limited amount is available on the home market, apart from the independent bottlers, but it is available overseas under the name Glen Isla.

OWNED BY
United Distillers plc

VISITORS
Reception Centre. Tel: 01496 840207

AGE AND STRENGTH WHEN BOTTLED
12 years old at 40% volume

COMMENTS
A very light-coloured, pleasing preprandial dram, not as round bodied as many on Islay, but with an attractive aftermath.

CAPERDONICH

SITUATION

Rothes, Morayshire. Grampian Region

CLASSIFICATION

Highland (Speyside)

ORIGINS AND BACKGROUND

In 1897 Major James Grant, son of Elgin lawyer James Grant, founder of the Glen Grant distillery at Rothes, decided to build a second distillery across the road from the first named Glen Grant 2, joining the two distilleries by a pipe, which mixed the two malts produced. Following the crash of the 1890s, the No. 2 distillery was closed down in 1901. It was rebuilt in 1965 and renamed the Caperdonich Distillery Ltd, using the name of the Caperdonich Well from which the water was obtained for the original Glen Grant distillery, and which has never been known to run dry.

OWNED BY

Seagram Distillers plc

VISITORS

By arrangement

AGE AND STRENGTH WHEN BOTTLED

Only available from the independent bottlers, so varies

COMMENTS

Similar, hardly surprisingly, to its neighbour Glen Grant, if perhaps not in quite the same class, although since it is rarely available it is hard to say. It seems to be a pleasing after-dinner dram with a good aftermath. It is a shame that it is not more readily available.

CARDHU *(car-doo)*

SITUATION

Knockando, Morayshire. Grampian Region

CLASSIFICATION

Highland (Speyside)

ORIGINS AND BACKGROUND

Founded in 1824 by John Cummings on a site where whisky had been distilled for many years illicitly. A second distillery close by was built in 1855, when the first had fallen into disrepair. It was bought by John Walker & Sons Ltd in 1893 and greatly expanded. Its water supply is piped from Mannoch Hill 2 miles to the northwest, and the distillery also gets its peat from the same site. It was extensively modernised in 1965 and the whisky is known as Cardhu. The distillery was often known as Cardow, which is merely a different spelling of the nearby hamlet sited on the banks of the Spey.

OWNED BY

United Distillers plc

VISITORS

Reception Centre. Tel: 01340 810204

AGE AND STRENGTH WHEN BOTTLED

12 years at 40% volume

COMMENTS

Smooth and clean with a good slightly sweet aftermath, this is a very sound after-dinner Speyside malt whisky.

Clynelish *(clyne-leesh)*

Situation
Brora, Sutherland. Highland Region

Classification
Highland (Northern)

Licensees
Ainslie & Heilbron (Distillers) Ltd

Origins and Background
Originally built in 1819 by the Duke of Sutherland, then Marquis of Stafford, to provide a market for the grain of the crofters forcibly moved to the coast as a result of the Clearances. It was originally called the Brora distillery and was sited next to the Brora coalfield to provide ready power, but the coal proved second-rate for the purpose, although the whisky distilled was highly regarded. Subsequently, in 1896, James Ainslie & Co. took over the distillery and completely rebuilt it about a mile farther away on the east coast. Despite the collapse of the whisky boom at the turn of the century, James Ainslie & Co. continued in business until 1912, when the DCL acquired a considerable shareholding. The Clynelish Distillery Co. Ltd was then formed and the distillery renamed. In 1925 DCL took over completely and built a new malt whisky distillery beside Clynelish, which was given the old name Brora, but it has since been dismantled and closed. It has now become a visitor centre.

Owned By
United Distillers plc

Visitors
Reception Centre. Tel: 01408 621444

Age and Strength When Bottled
12 years at 40% volume

Comments
A rather peaty and very interesting after-dinner dram with an extremely good aftermath.

COLEBURN

SITUATION

Longmorn, by Elgin, Morayshire. Grampian Region

CLASSIFICATION

Highland (Speyside)

ORIGINS AND BACKGROUND

The distillery was built in 1896 by John Robertson & Son Ltd, trying like many others to cash in on the seemingly ever upwards spiral of the Scotch whisky boom of the '90s. During the early years of the present century, the distillery was the subject for several successful experiments in the purification of industrial effluents. The process developed at Coleburn was utilised in a number of distilleries elsewhere in the area. The distillery was taken over in 1916 by the Clynelish Distillery Co. Ltd, and in 1930 it was acquired by the Scottish Malt Distillers Ltd, a subsidiary of the DCL. The malt produced was mostly used for distilling but some was bottled independently by Wm Cadenhead Ltd. It has been closed for some years.

OWNED BY

United Distillers plc

VISITORS

No

AGE AND STRENGTH WHEN BOTTLED

Only available through the independent bottlers

COMMENTS

In view of the proximity of such a rare malt whisky as Longmorn, it is a pity this is not bottled by the distillery. Judging by the independent bottlings, it seems an interesting light and clean-tasting dram, but not up to its neighbour's standards.

CRAGGANMORE

SITUATION
Ballindalloch, Banffshire. Grampian Region

CLASSIFICATION
Highland (Speyside)

ORIGINS AND BACKGROUND
Built in 1869 by John Smith, who had left his employer at The Glenlivet Distillery to branch out as a self-employed farmer and distiller on his own account. A man of considerable strength and magnificent physique, he is reputed to have moved a large stone that stands at the entrance to the distillery by his own efforts when it obstructed his plough. In the course of so doing he uncovered a hidden treasure and flourished exceedingly thereafter. His son Gordon Smith inherited the distillery from his father and on his death in 1923 it was sold to a syndicate, who formed the Cragganmore Distillery Co. Ltd. A leading member of the syndicate was Peter J. Mackie, later Sir Peter Mackie, of White Horse Distillers Ltd. In 1965 the remaining shareholders were bought out and the distillery was taken over by the DCL, hence is now part of United Distillers plc.

OWNED BY
United Distillers plc

VISITORS
No

AGE AND STRENGTH WHEN BOTTLED
12 years at 40% volume

COMMENTS
Although the bulk still goes for blending, it is now readily available and marketed as one of United Distillers' six Classic Malts. It is a good dry and demanding after-dinner dram, possibly more west coast in character rather than typically Speyside.

Craigellachie

Situation
Craigellachie, Banffshire. Grampian Region

Classification
Highland (Speyside)

Origins and Background
Built in 1890 by Peter J. Mackie in partnership with Alexander Edward, as the Craigellachie-Glenlivet Distillery Ltd, but eventually taken over completely by Peter Mackie. It stands impressively above the well-known single-span Craigellachie bridge across the River Spey and the Craigellachie Rock. When Mackie & Co., Distillers, Ltd, were taken over in 1924 by the DCL to be transformed into White Horse Distillers Limited, the distillery became part of the DCL empire.

Owned by
United Distillers plc

Visitors
No

Age and Strength when Bottled
14 years at 43% volume

Comments
This is another single malt that United Distillers are now bottling and selling on a limited basis. It seems a light and clean after-dinner dram.

DALUAINE

SITUATION
Carron, Morayshire. Grampian Region

CLASSIFICATION
Highland (Speyside)

ORIGINS AND BACKGROUND
The distillery was built in the shadow of Ben Rinnes in 1852, but was completely renovated and rebuilt at the start of the whisky boom in the early 1890s by Thomas Mackenzie. A merger between Daluaine-Glenlivet Distillers Ltd and Talisker Distillery Ltd in 1898 led to the formation of the Daluaine-Talisker Distilleries Ltd. They were acquired in 1916 jointly by Dewar, DCL, W. P. Lowrie, and Johnnie Walker, before all came under the DCL umbrella in 1925.

OWNED BY
United Distillers plc

VISITORS
No

AGE AND STRENGTH WHEN BOTTLED
16 years at 43% volume

COMMENTS
Yet another single malt that United Distillers are now bottling on a limited scale. It provides an extremely interesting smooth dram that is well worth making an effort to find.

DALMORE

SITUATION
Alness, Ross-shire. Highland Region

CLASSIFICATION
Highland (Northern)

ORIGINS AND BACKGROUND
Splendidly placed overlooking the Black Isle and the Cromarty Firth, with the sole rights to take water from the River Alness, the Dalmore distillery was founded in 1839 and was taken over by Mackenzie Brothers in 1867, still the present owners. Although they merged with Whyte & Mackay Ltd in 1960, they had a Mackenzie of the third generation serving on the board until 1988. Although one of the stills in use dates back to 1874, the distillery has a record of adopting modern methods of production and its capacity is 1.2 million gallons, or 3.114 million litres of alcohol. During the World War the distillery was taken over by the Royal Navy for the assembling of mines and because of this did not start distilling again until 1922. The bulk of the malt goes to make up Whyte & Mackay's blends, but some is bottled.

OWNED BY
Whyte & Mackay Distillers Ltd

VISITORS
Reception Centre. Tel: 01349 882362

AGE AND STRENGTH WHEN BOTTLED
12 years at 40% volume

COMMENTS
A rather dry but very pleasing, heavy, after-dinner dram with an interesting aftermath.

Dalwhinnie

Situation

Dalwhinnie, Inverness-shire. Highland Region

Classification

Highland (Central)

Origins and Background

Sited in the Pass of Drumochter, the distillery was built in 1898 by Alex Mackenzie and George Sellar of Kingussie at a height of 1,174 feet and it was then claimed to be the highest distillery in Scotland. The Gaelic meaning of Dalwhinnie is "the meeting place" and it is certainly an area that has lived up to its name over the centuries. Historically it has seen clan battles and Prince Charles's army encamped after the raising of the standard at Glenfinnan in 1745 as he marched down General Wade's military road, which runs through the distillery grounds. The distillery was taken over from the founders by A. P. Blyth & Son, who sold it in 1905 to James Munro & Son Ltd, an American syndicate. In 1921 it was sold to Sir James Calder and in 1926 was taken over by J & G Stewart Ltd, but in 1930 went to the Scottish Malt Distillers Ltd, under DCL control. Mostly used for blending but recently promoted successfully as a malt whisky.

Owned By

United Distillers plc

Visitors

Reception Centre. Tel: 01528 522208

Age and Strength When Bottled

15 years at 43% volume

Comments

Now well marketed and widely available, this is a fresh but very smooth malt whisky with a good clean aftermath. A pleasant preprandial dram.

Deanston

Situation

Doune, Perthshire. Tayside Region

Classification

Highland (Southern)

Origins and Background

Built on the site of an old cotton mill on the banks of the River Teith and named after the nearby village of Deanston, it is about a mile from the picturesque Castle Doune. Although it is near to the river, which is good for salmon, the water for the distilling process comes from the Trossachs. The cotton mill dates back to 1785, but when James Finlay & Co. Ltd, the mill-owners, moved elsewhere in 1965, Mr Brodie Hepburn, well known in the whisky industry, saw the potential. Here were large premises well placed on the River Teith, with a water turbine and standby generator in working order. He suggested the idea of converting them into a distillery to James Finlay & Co. A deal was agreed whereby James Finlay took two-thirds of the equity and Brodie Hepburn Ltd the remainder and overall control. Two wash- and two spirit-stills were installed and in 1969 production started. Then in 1972 Deanston Distillers Ltd were taken over by Invergordon Distillers Ltd. In 1991 they were sold to Burn Stewart & Co. Ltd. The distillery has a capacity of 750,000 proof gallons a year, or 1,946,250 litres of alcohol.

Owned By

Burn Stewart & Co. Ltd

Visitors

By arrangement. Tel: 01786 841422

Age and Strength When Bottled

12, 17, and 25 years old at 40% volume

Comments

A light predinner dram clean, fresh, and a touch sweet.

DUFFTOWN-GLENLIVET

SITUATION
Highland (Speyside)

ORIGINS AND BACKGROUND
Built in 1896 by P. Mackenzie & Co., Distillers, Ltd, just to the south of Dufftown in the Dullan Glen, this is another distillery using the hyphenated Glenlivet affix. Despite the fact that the Dullan and Fiddich Burns both flow down the Dullan Glen to the Spey, it obtains its water supplies from "Jock's Well," regarded as ideal for distilling purposes and noted for its never-failing supply of fine water. In 1933 the distillery was acquired by Arthur Bell & Sons Ltd, at the start of their steady expansion, and this was to become one of the principal sources of their popular blend. Now a subsidiary of United Distillers plc.

OWNED BY
United Distillers plc

VISITORS
No

AGE AND STRENGTH WHEN BOTTLED
8 and 10 years at 40% volume

COMMENTS
A light but smooth, very typical Speyside malt whisky and a good aperitif. The 8-year-old, hardly surprisingly, is not quite up to the standard of the 10-year-old. They may feel they need the Glenlivet affix, but both are sound enough on their own merits.

EDRADOUR

SITUATION
Pitlochry, Perthshire. Tayside Region

CLASSIFICATION
Highland (Southern)

ORIGINS AND BACKGROUND
Believed to have been founded around 1825 by a group of local farmers, the present distillery was probably built around 1837. It was owned by John McIntosh & Co. for many years until finally sold to William Whiteley & Co. Ltd in 1933. In 1938 this company was acquired by a Mr Irving Haim, an American, and remained in his hands for 40 years. In 1978 control passed to Mr Delbert Coleman, an American financier, whose holding company was J. G. Turney Ltd. The distillery was then purchased by Pernod Ricard through their subsidiary S. Campbell & Son Ltd, and they are the current owners. It lies beside a burn with steep banks on land leased from the Duke of Atholl. It is widely regarded as the prettiest distillery in Scotland and is certainly the smallest. The spirit-still holds under 500 gallons and production rarely exceeds 1,000 gallons a week. More than almost any distillery, it resembles the way a Highland distillery was worked in the 19th century. It only employs four men, but they manage the entire operation efficiently and smoothly, making this distillery a pleasure to visit. Messrs Pernod Ricard are to be congratulated on not having made any alterations to this showpiece distillery.

OWNED BY
Ricard International SA

VISITORS
Reception Centre. Tel: 01796 472095

AGE AND STRENGTH WHEN BOTTLED
10 years at 40%

COMMENTS
A good, clean, smooth and light malt whisky with a pleasing aftermath, also bottled by the independent bottlers.

FETTERCAIRN

SITUATION

Fettercairn, Kincardineshire. Grampian Region

CLASSIFICATION

Highland (Eastern)

ORIGINS AND BACKGROUND

The exact date of origin is uncertain, but the present distillery was known to be functioning in 1824 and continued distilling under various owners until it was taken over by a local landowner, Sir John Gladstone, brother of the Prime Minister. Sir John formed the Fettercairn Distillery Co. in 1887. It underwent a long period of closure from the First World War onward until it was bought by the Associated Scottish Distillers Ltd in 1939 for Train & McIntyre. It then passed to Mr Tom Scott Sutherland, an Aberdonian businessman, who retained it until 1971, when it was purchased jointly by Hay and MacLeod & Co. and W. & S. Strong & Co. It is now an up-to-date modern distillery with water in plenty from the nearby Grampian Mountains, and situated in the fertile Howe o' the Mearns it has plentiful barley supplies at hand. The capacity is about 500,000 proof gallons. The malt whisky produced is known as Old Fettercairn. The bulk goes for blending, but some is bottled.

OWNED BY

Whyte & Mackay Distillers Ltd

VISITORS

Reception Centre. Tel: 01561 340244

AGE AND STRENGTH WHEN BOTTLED

10 years at 43% volume

COMMENTS

A good, clean, dry and satisfying malt whisky that makes a pleasing dram before dinner.

GLEN DEVERON: *see* MACDUFF

GLEN ELGIN

SITUATION
Longmorn, Elgin, Morayshire. Grampian Region

CLASSIFICATION
Highland (Speyside)

ORIGINS AND BACKGROUND
It cannot be often that bankers get together to found a distillery, and it is entirely suitable that this should happen on Speyside, where banking, salmon, and whisky might all be considered local industries. In 1900 Mr James Carle and Mr W. Simpson, both bankers in Elgin, founded this distillery at Longmorn near Glen Rothes in as pleasant a position as any in the Highlands. It obtains its water supplies from springs in Glen Rothes. The Glen Elgin- Glenlivet Distillery Co. Ltd, another hyphenated Glenlivet distillery company, was formed to run the venture. Then in 1907 J. J. Blanche of Glasgow took over the company, but in 1936 it was finally acquired by the Scottish Malt Distillers.

OWNED BY
United Distillers plc

VISITORS
By arrangement. Tel: 01343 860212

AGE AND STRENGTH WHEN BOTTLED
12 years at 43% volume

COMMENTS
The bulk is used for blending, but some is regularly bottled and sold. It is a typical, clean Speyside dram with a light but pleasing aftermath. This is a good single malt whisky that may be drunk at any time with enjoyment.

GLEN ESK

SITUATION
Hillside, Montrose, Angus. Grampian Region

CLASSIFICATION
Highland (Eastern)

ORIGINS AND BACKGROUND
This distillery has changed its name more often than most. It was built in 1897 at the height of the whisky boom by a firm with the unlikely name of Septimus Parsonage & Co. Ltd. It was then known as the Highland Esk Distillery. It was soon acquired by a firm of distillers called Heddle and was renamed the North Esk. It was damaged by fire in 1910, but rebuilt, only to be closed during the 1914–18 War. After the war, in 1919 it was acquired by Thomas Bernard & Co. and used as a maltings. In 1938 it was bought by Associated Scottish Distilleries Ltd, and turned into a patent-still grain distillery, known as the Montrose Distillery. In 1954 it was acquired by the DCL and returned once more to malt whisky distilling in 1965, at this stage being renamed Hillside. Finally in 1980 the name was once more changed to Glenesk. The whisky is mostly used for blending but is also bottled at 12 years. It is currently closed. Now known as Glen Esk.

OWNED BY
United Distillers plc

VISITORS
No

AGE AND STRENGTH WHEN BOTTLED
12 years at 40% volume

COMMENTS
A sound, faintly sweetish after-dinner dram with a clean dry aftermath, but is now only available from the independent bottlers.

GLEN GARIOCH *(glen-geery)*

SITUATION

Old Meldrum, Aberdeenshire, Grampian Region

CLASSIFICATION

Highland (Eastern)

ORIGINS AND BACKGROUND

Reputedly founded in the 1790s in the village of Old Meldrum, 20 miles northwest of Aberdeen, the distillery was bought by J. F. Thomson & Co of Leith in 1840 and in the 1860s was acquired by Wm Sanderson & Son, Ltd., blenders of the famous Vat 69. In 1937 it was taken over by DCL, but due to continual water shortages and with a working capacity of only 140,000 gallons was closed in 1968. In 1970 it was sold to Stanley P. Morrison Ltd of Glasgow, who sank a deep well nearby, tapping an entirely new source of water. With peat from Pitsligo Moss and with a new wash-still in 1973, it has been distilling 500,000 proof gallons annually, or 1,297,500 litres of alcohol. Waste-heat from the distillery heats glasshouses growing fruits and vegetables.

OWNED BY

Morrison Bowmore Distillers Co. Ltd

VISITORS

Reception Centre: Tel: 01651 872706

AGE AND STRENGTH WHEN BOTTLED

10 and 12 years at 40%; 15 and 21 years at 43% volume

COMMENTS

The 10-year-old is a good sound dram to be recommended at any time. The 12- and 15-year-olds each improve with age. The 21-year-old is a smooth, full-bodied, peaty malt with a fine aftermath.

GLEN GRANT

SITUATION

Rothes, Morayshire. Grampian Region

CLASSIFICATION

Highland (Speyside)

ORIGINS AND BACKGROUND

There has to be something special about the professional men of Elgin and for that matter the name Grant as well, for it was an Elgin lawyer, James Grant, who in partnership with his younger brother, John, in 1840 founded the Glen Grant distillery on the banks of the Glen Grant Burn near the village of Rothes. They had admittedly been distilling at nearby Dandaleith since 1834, so they knew what they were about, and it was not long before they were enlarging their new distillery and producing 40,000 gallons a year. The introduction of the railway line, which the Grant family did much to encourage, was a great step forward from the transport by horse to the coast and allowed them to expand considerably. The distillery was already a very successful concern when Major James Grant took over control on his father's death in 1872. It was he who decided to expand by building another distillery in 1897 across the road from the original one and joined by a pipe. Called initially Glen Grant No. 2, this was eventually renamed Caperdonich. (See **Caperdonich.**) The company, by this time known as J. & J. Grant, Glen Grant Ltd, merged in 1932 with George and J. G. Smith Ltd to form The Glenlivet and Glen Grant Distilleries Ltd. In 1970 they merged with Hill Thomson & Co. Ltd and Longmorn-Glenlivet Distilleries Ltd, the name of the merged company being rationalised to The Glenlivet Distillers Ltd. Finally, in 1978, they were in turn taken over by Seagram Distillers plc.

OWNED BY

Seagram Distillers plc

VISITORS

Reception Centre and Museum—on the Whisky Trail. Tel: 01542 783318

AGE AND STRENGTH WHEN BOTTLED

No age given at 40% volume, 5 years old at 40% volume, and 10 years at 43% volume

COMMENTS

This excellent malt whisky used to be bottled and readily available at 5, 10, and 15 years. Unfortunately, it has become too popular, selling over 500,000 cases of 5-year-old annually in Italy alone. Stock availability has dictated that it is now quite hard to find at any age. It is, however, a favourite amongst the independent bottlers, so all is not lost. The first noted above with no age given is a good dry dram. The second at 5 years old is a pale-coloured light and tasty dram that one can understand being popular in Italy and anywhere else. The 10-year-old is a medium light, very dry, and satisfactory malt whisky. Some of the independent bottlings are excellent.

GLEN ISLA: *see* CAOL ISLA

GLEN KEITH

SITUATION

Keith, Banffshire. Grampian Region

CLASSIFICATION

Highland (Speyside)

ORIGINS AND BACKGROUND

In 1957 Seagram Distillers plc bought a flour mill from the Angus Milling Co. Ltd, facing their Strathisla Distillery on the other bank of the River Isla. After a year's intensive programme of rebuilding, a new distillery was opened on the site in 1958. This was the first distillery in Scotland to use gas-fired stills in place of the traditional coal-fired stills. The water for distilling is obtained from the Newmill Spring and peat comes from Knockando. Originally called the Glenkeith-Glenlivet distillery on the acquisition of The Glenlivet Distillers, the affix was dropped by Seagram. Although previously it was all used for blending with only a little bottled by independent bottlers, Seagram, like United Distillers, have now appreciated that it is worth bottling and selling their own single malts, and Glen Keith is now generally available.

OWNED BY

Seagram Distillers plc

VISITORS

By arrangement. Tel: 01542 783002

AGE AND STRENGTH WHEN BOTTLED

10 years at 43% volume

COMMENTS

Although most is still used for blending, this addition to the generally available single malts is well worth bottling. Other distillers, who have not yet done so, should take note. This is a pleasant dram before or after a meal.

GLEN MORAY

SITUATION
Elgin, Morayshire. Grampian Region

CLASSIFICATION
Highland (Speyside)

ORIGINS AND BACKGROUND
The site of this distillery, founded in 1897 towards the end of the whisky boom, was originally that of the town's West Brewery owned by Henry Arnot & Co. Unfortunately, very little appears to have been recorded of its early history until 1920, when it was acquired by Macdonald & Muir Ltd, by which time it had already been closed for a lengthy period. In 1958 the entire distillery underwent a considerable amount of development and enlargement, and it now has a capacity of 700,000 gallons a year, or 1,764,000 litres of alcohol. It has also now dropped the Glenlivet affix on its bottlings. Although a great deal is used for blending, some is kept aside for bottling at 12 years.

OWNED BY
Macdonald Martin Distilleries plc

VISITORS
Reception centre. Tel: 01343 860577

AGE AND STRENGTH WHEN BOTTLED
12 years at 40% volume

COMMENTS
This 12-year-old makes a very good, clean, mellow, all-around dram. It is a good, sound example of a light dry Speyside malt whisky.

Glen Ord

Situation
Muir of Ord, Beauly. Highland Region

Classification
Highland (Northern)

Origins and Background
The area was notorious for illicit distilling even as late as the end of the 19th century, and there is little doubt that the distillery was built on the site of an old illicit still, but it was only licensed in 1838. Ample water supplies are available from Glen Oran and the Oran Burn, making illicit distilling easy. The holder of the first license was a Mr McLennan. When he died, his widow married an Alexander McKenzie, who thus acquired the distillery as well. It was then acquired by John Watson & Co. Ltd, of Dundee, and finally in 1924 was bought by John Dewar just prior to their takeover by the DCL. It is notable that heather is mixed with the peat during the malt-drying process and the taste of the malt probably owes something to this. Although much goes for blending, it is also bottled by the distillers, but no longer marketed under the names Ord or Glenordie, as used to be the case. It is now sold as Glen Ord at 12 years old.

Owned By
United Distillers plc

Visitors
Reception centre. Tel: 01463 870421

Age and Strength When Bottled
12 years old at 40% volume

Comments
A good dry and full-bodied malt whisky with a clean aftermath well worth drinking at any time.

GLEN SCOTIA

SITUATION
Campbeltown. Strathclyde Region

CLASSIFICATION
Campbeltown (West Coast)

ORIGINS AND BACKGROUND
The distillery was built by the Galbraith family in 1832, close to the Parliament Square in the centre of Campbeltown, and was at first named the Scotia. With ample water, peat, coal, and barley available locally, during the 19th century it was one of the 34 distilleries that provided the small town with the proud boast that it was "the whisky capital of Scotland." Indifferent distilling and the sale of immature whiskies gave the area a bad name with disastrous results. The Glen Scotia distillery is now one of the only two left. It was owned by A. Gillies & Co. Ltd, but was acquired by Barton International plc, then passed to the Loch Lomond Distillery Co. Ltd, who also own Littlemill, where it is planned to mature most of the production from Glen Scotia.

OWNED BY
Loch Lomond Distillery Co. Ltd

VISITORS
By arrangement. Tel: 01389 874154 (Littlemill)

AGE AND STRENGTH WHEN BOTTLED
14 years old at 40% volume

COMMENTS
The malt whisky produced by Glen Scotia has a rich, peaty, slightly oily taste with an affinity to Irish whiskey but with a strong and interesting aftermath, making a good dram at any time.

Glen Spey

Situation
Rothes, Morayshire. Grampian Region

Classification
Highland (Speyside)

Origins and Background
This distillery was built originally in 1885 by James Stuart and was then known as the Mills of Rothes with the intention of milling cereals, but he found that whisky distilling was more profitable and converted the operation. However, his heart does not seem to have been in it, for two years later he sold out to the Gilbey brothers, Walter and Alfred, who although starting out as wine merchants and progressing to gin distilling had early on appreciated the potential of whisky distilling. Now part of International Distillers and Vintners Ltd, since 1962, the distillery has a capacity of 750,000 proof gallons, almost all of which goes for blending, although some no doubt forms part of the vatted malt Strathspey marketed by the parent company. It used to add the Glenlivet affix, but this has now been dropped. Currently none is bottled.

Owned By
International Distillers and Vintners Ltd

Visitors
By arrangement

Age and Strength When Bottled
8 years at 40% volume

Comments
Bottled at 8 years and 40% volume, this malt whisky is clearly from Speyside, making a pleasant, very smooth preprandial dram.

Glenallachie

Situation
Aberlour, Banffshire. Grampian Region

Classification
Highland (Speyside)

Origins and Background
This distillery was built in the mini-boom years of the 1960s. The architect who designed it, Mr Delme Evans, also designed two others, one on the Isle of Jura above Islay and the other at Tullibardine in Perthshire. It can be no coincidence that Glenallachie and Isle of Jura were both then owned by Scottish and Newcastle Breweries Ltd, who obviously liked his work on their Isle of Jura distillery in 1958. Taken over in 1985 by Invergordon Distillers and then temporarily closed, it was acquired later by Pernod Ricard.

Owned By
Ricard International SA

Visitors
By arrangement

Age and Strength When Bottled
12 years at 40% volume

Comments
A pleasing, smooth, light dram that is best drunk before dinner when the subtle fragrance of the aftermath can be fully savoured.

GLENBURGIE

SITUATION
Forres, Morayshire. Grampian Region

CLASSIFICATION
Highland (Speyside)

ORIGINS AND BACKGROUND
This is another distillery that can lay claim to being among the oldest in the Highlands, since it is said to have been established in 1810 by William Paul with a modest capacity of 90 gallons. It changed hands a number of times during the 19th century and each change of ownership appears to have resulted in an increase in its capacity, so that when it was taken over by Alexander Fraser & Co. in the 1890s the wash-still had a capacity of 1,500 gallons. The distillery was subsequently acquired by James & George Stodart Ltd of Dumbarton, who were themselves taken over by Hiram Walker (Scotland) Ltd, in 1930, in their first venture into the Scotch Whisky industry. Two spirit-stills and two wash-stills were also added in 1958, but removed in 1980. For a while the whisky produced from them was known as Glencraig. Any malt whisky bottled is marketed as Glenburgie-Glenlivet.

OWNED BY
Allied Distillers Ltd

VISITORS
By arrangement. Tel: 01343 850258

AGE AND STRENGTH WHEN BOTTLED
Only bottled by the independent bottlers

COMMENTS
On the evidence available it is a fairly typical light Speyside malt whisky and as such a good dram. It is notable that although twenty miles from Glenlivet, the firm still finds the use of the hyphenated Glenlivet affix worthwhile.

Glencadam

Situation
Brechin, Angus. Tayside Region

Classification
Highland (Eastern)

Origins and Background
Situated in a steep-sided glen, the distillery obtains ample water supplies from the Moorfoot Loch. It was first licensed in 1825 and, as with many around this date, was almost certainly built on the site of a previously illicit still. It went through a number of changes of ownership until acquired in 1891 by Gilmour Thomson & Co. Ltd. The distillery was finally bought by Hiram Walker and Sons (Scotland) Ltd in 1954, as another acquisition in their expanding empire. The whisky almost all goes for blending, but may be obtained from the independent bottlers.

Owned By
Allied Distillers Ltd

Visitors
By arrangement. Tel: 01356 622217

Age and Strength When Bottled
Varies as only obtainable from the independent bottlers

Comments
On a sample tasted aged 14 years and 46% it would seem to be a good after-dinner malt worthwhile bottling by the distillery.

GLENDRONACH

SITUATION

Forgue, by Huntly, Aberdeenshire. Grampian Region

CLASSIFICATION

Highland (Speyside)

ORIGINS AND BACKGROUND

The distillery was built in 1826 by James Allardyce and a syndicate of local businessmen. Unfortunately, disagreements and financial losses through mismanagement in the early years were followed by an extensive fire in 1837, after which the distillery was taken over by Mr Walter Scott. Its history thereafter was fairly straightforward. It takes its name and water from the Dronac Burn. It was acquired by Captain Charles Grant, one of the Grants of the Glenfiddich distilling family, until it was sold to William Teacher & Sons Ltd in 1960, when it was considerably enlarged. It retained certain old-fashioned features such as floor maltings and coal-fired pot-stills, but was extensively modernised. Until then it had used the hyphenated Glenlivet prefix, but this was dropped. Local control is in the hands of the Glendronach Distillery Company Limited, Huntly, and comparatively recently production has doubled.

OWNED BY

Allied Distillers Ltd

VISITORS

Reception centre. Tel: 01466 730202

AGE AND STRENGTH WHEN BOTTLED

12 years at 40% volume

COMMENTS

Comes as the Original, aged in oak and sherry wood casks, or the Sherrywood, aged in sherry wood casks. Favoured in Aberdeenshire. The Original is a touch peppery initially, but both are good after-dinner drams with a distinctive long, dry aftermath.

GLENDULLAN

SITUATION
Dufftown, Banffshire. Grampian Region

CLASSIFICATION
Highland (Speyside)

ORIGINS AND BACKGROUND
This distillery was built by William Williams & Sons Ltd of Aberdeen at the height of the whisky boom in 1896 at Dufftown, making the seventh distillery ringing the town. William Williams & Sons Ltd were whisky blenders and merchants who used most of the malt whisky produced at Glendullan for their blends, although some was bottled as a malt whisky of sufficient distinction to acquire a Royal Warrant in 1902 as supplied to King Edward VII. During the 1914–18 War they merged with Macdonald Greenlees and formed Macdonald Greenlees and Williams (Distillers) Ltd, being subsequently acquired by the DCL. At one time the hyphenated Glenlivet addition to the name was used and it was marketed as Glendullan-Glenlivet, but this practice has now ceased.

OWNED BY
United Distillers plc

VISITORS
No

AGE AND STRENGTH WHEN BOTTLED
12 years at 43% volume

COMMENTS
A smooth dram with a good aftermath, this makes a good after-dinner Speyside malt whisky that deserves to be better known.

GLENFARCLAS

SITUATION

Marypark, Ballindalloch, Banffshire. Grampian Region

CLASSIFICATION

Highland (Speyside)

ORIGINS AND BACKGROUND

Built in 1836 by Robert Hay, this distillery was purchased in 1865 by John Grant, the first of five generations of the Grant family who have owned the distillery. Initially he sub-let the distillery to John Smith, the noted distiller at the nearby Glenlivet Distillery, who already had established a notable reputation. It is not surprising, therefore, that the affix Glenlivet was added onto the Glenfarclas name. John Grant took over full control of the distillery in 1870. During the 1880s he handed over increasing control to his son George, and died in 1889. George unfortunately died prematurely in 1890, when his wife took over control and managed the business successfully until their sons, John and George, were old enough to take over themselves in 1895. In that year they formed The Glenfarclas-Glenlivet Distillery Co. Ltd, on an equal share basis with the Leith blenders Pattison, Elder & Co., whose spectacular bankruptcy in 1898 signalled the end of the whisky boom. Thereafter, the Grant family remained in full control of the distillery. John Grant retired from the partnership after the 1914–18 War, but George remained in sole control until 1947, when he formed J. & G. Grant Ltd. On his death in 1949 the distillery went to his sons George Scott Grant and John P. Grant. The latter died in 1960, but the family remains in control of the distillery. As one of his first actions in 1896, at the height of the whisky boom, George Grant had instituted considerable rebuilding and renovations that brought the production up to nearly 300,000 proof gallons a year, or 778,500 litres of alcohol. It is indicative of the long depression in the industry that it was not until 1960 that considerable rebuilding and modernisation finally doubled the capacity to 600,000 gallons, or 1,557,000 litres of alcohol. Since then the annual capacity has been raised yet again to a million gallons, or 2.595 million litres of alcohol. Clearly finding no need for it any longer, the Glenfarclas Distillery has now dropped the affix Glenlivet and reverted to its original name.

OWNED BY

J. & G. Grant Ltd

VISITORS

Reception centre—on the Whisky Trail. Tel: 01807 500257

AGE AND STRENGTH WHEN BOTTLED

8 years at 40% and 60% volume; 12 years at 43% volume; 15 years at 46% volume; 21 years at 43% volume

COMMENTS

With nearly 125 years of the same family in control, this must be unique even in an industry where tradition and continuity count for a great deal. This is a malt whisky of character, and Glenfarclas makes a very fine after-dinner dram at any age and strength.

Glenfiddich

Situation
Dufftown, Banffshire. Grampian Region

Classification
Highland (Speyside)

Origins and Background
The founding of this distillery, like that of Glenfarclas, is very much a family story relating yet again to the name Grant, itself amongst the most notable and frequently found wherever Scotch whisky is distilled. Although starting some 20 years after the Grants of Glenfarclas, the Grants of Glenfiddich made up for matters by sheer numbers. In 1886 William Grant, who already had 20 years' experience of distilling in the Mortlach distillery, bought the land on the Robbie Dubh spring nearby. He also bought the old disused plant from the Cardow distillery, which was then being re-equipped for £120, and set about building his own distillery, using water for cooling purposes from the nearby Fiddich Burn from which the distillery gained its name of Glenfiddich. With the aid of his seven sons and his entire capital of £755, he had the distillery producing whisky by 1887 and was so successful that in five years he was building Balvenie close at hand.

Thereafter, expansion was steady with the formation of a limited company, William Grant & Sons Ltd, in 1903, with which William Grant remained actively involved until his death in 1923. Meanwhile, Captain Charles Grant, one of his sons, had taken over the Glendronach distillery (sold to William Teacher in 1960, see **Glendronach**) and in the post 1939–45 boom years the firm, still very much a family concern, built a grain distillery at Girvan in Ayrshire, near which they built a Lowland malt distillery named Ladyburn, used entirely for blending. The success of their blend Grant's Standfast, which owed much to skilful marketing, was followed in the 1960s by the widespread foreign sales and marketing of the Glenfiddich, the first determinedly successful overseas sales of a malt whisky, gaining a Queen's

Award to Industry for Export Achievement in 1974. Still very much a family company, William Grant & Sons Ltd continue to manage Glenfiddich and the neighbouring Balvenie distilleries as well as the Girvan plant and their worldwide blending marketing projects with determination and flair, while Grants are still prominent in the board of directors, the grandsons and great-grandsons of William and his progeny. It is a remarkable success story by any standards.

OWNED BY

William Grant & Sons Ltd

VISITORS

Reception centre—on the Whisky Trail. Tel: 01340 820373

AGE AND STRENGTH WHEN BOTTLED

No age given at 40% volume; 18, 21, and 30 years at 43% volume.

COMMENTS

With their widespread overseas sales and their reception centre at Glenfiddich distillery, the former must be amongst the malt whiskies most frequently drunk for the first time. At least 8 years old, it makes a good light introduction to malt whisky that should interest and encourage those who have not drunk any previously. Also available at 18, 21, and 30 years old at 43% volume and improves with each. With the latter two, a presentation decanter is included.

Glenglassaugh

SITUATION
Portsoy, Banffshire. Grampian Region

CLASSIFICATION
Highland (Speyside)

ORIGINS AND BACKGROUND
This distillery was built in 1875 about a couple of miles along the coast from the small fishing village of Portsoy, 6½ miles west of Banff itself. It obtains its water from local springs close to the site. The Highland Distilleries acquired it in 1892 and still own it. They completely rebuilt and renovated it in 1959 so that it had an output of 1.2 million litres of alcohol, mostly used for blending, although some was bottled by the distillery and the independent bottlers. The distillery is currently closed.

OWNED BY
The Highland Distilleries Co. plc

VISITORS
No

AGE AND STRENGTH WHEN BOTTLED
12 years at 40% volume

COMMENTS
This is a pleasant, slightly sweetish dram but with a dry aftermath that deserves to be more easily available.

GLENGOYNE

SITUATION

Dumgoyne, Stirlingshire (2 miles southeast of Killearn). Tayside Region

CLASSIFICATION

Highland (Southwestern)

ORIGINS AND BACKGROUND

Sited in a wooded glen at the foot of Dumgoyne Hill, the water supply comes from the nearby Campsie Fells. This is a particularly attractively placed distillery and is also a very suitable one for visitors who want to see the whole process without too much walking. It is also very convenient for Glasgow. First licensed to Archibald McLellan in 1833, it was then known as the Glenguin distillery. When it was taken over by the brothers Alexander and Gavin Lang in 1876, it was renamed the Glengoyne distillery. Lang Brothers Ltd were themselves taken over by Robertson & Baxter Ltd in 1965, and the distillery was then completely modernised.

OWNED BY

Lang Brothers Ltd

VISITORS

Reception centre. Tel: 01360 550254

AGE AND STRENGTH WHEN BOTTLED

10 years at 40% volume; 12 and 17 years at 43% volume

COMMENTS

Situated right on the imaginary Highland Line, it may be classified as a southern Highland malt whisky, but regardless of position the 10-year-old is a light, clean, and pleasant dram. The 12-year-old is rather more mature and smoother and the 17-year-old even more so. In effect, like many malt whiskies, it changes with age from a good pre-dinner dram to a good after-dinner dram.

GLENKINCHIE

SITUATION
Glenkinchie, Pencaitland, East Lothian. Lothian Region

CLASSIFICATION
Lowland (Eastern)

ORIGINS AND BACKGROUND
Built somewhere around 1837 by a local farmer named John Rate, it was subsequently sold to another East Lothian farmer named Christie, who bought it not for distilling, but for use as a sawmill and cattle shed. In 1880 it was sold again, to a syndicate interested in turning it back into a distillery. In 1890, as the whisky boom developed, they formed the Glenkinchie Distillery Company. In 1914 it was taken over by the Scottish Malt Distillers Ltd, since when it has been considerably modernised and rebuilt. Most of the whisky still goes for blending, but now that control has passed to United Distillers, it is also readily available as a single malt whisky.

OWNED BY
United Distillers plc

VISITORS
Reception centre and museum. Tel: 01875 340451. Popular as the nearest to Edinburgh

AGE AND STRENGTH WHEN BOTTLED
10 years old and 43% volume when bottled by the distillery

COMMENTS
There is an attractive dryness about this distinctively Lowland malt whisky, making a good clean dram with a smooth aftermath. With the demise of Bladnoch, Kinclaith, and Ladyburn, this is now the southernmost Lowland distillery and happily the 10-year-old malt is widely available as another of United Distillers' six Classic Malts.

The Glenlivet

SITUATION
Minmore, Banffshire. Grampian Region

CLASSIFICATION
Highland (Speyside)

ORIGINS AND BACKGROUND
It is well known that George Smith founded the Glenlivet Distillery in 1824. His ancestors appear to have been first recorded in that then wild and desolate area of the Highlands in 1715 at the time of the first Jacobite rising. Although Thomas Smith, George's great-grandfather, was probably out with his Laird in the 1715 rebellion, he does not appear to have supported the Jacobites in the 1745 Rising. It may have been because of this that he and his family appear to have escaped any of the draconian punishments imposed by the Duke of Cumberland after the '45.

By the time Thomas's great-grandson, George Smith, took over from his father, Andrew, in 1817 at Upper Drumin as one of the Duke of Gordon's tenants, illicit Glenlivet whisky was known and popular as far south as Edinburgh. It was George who first took out a license in 1824 under the Act of 1823 with the Duke's encouragement and started distilling legally, in the face of fierce opposition from his erstwhile friends who still continued to distil illicitly. It was thus in 1824 that the distillery at Upper Drumin was amongst the first distilleries to distil legally with a capacity of 50 gallons weekly that by 1839 had risen dramatically four times to 200 gallons a week. With his son-in-law Captain William Grant distilling at nearby Auchorachan, George Smith maintained that only they could distil whisky with the title Glenlivet, but in 1850 William Grant died and his distillery ceased operations. However, George Smith then built another distillery at Delnabo near Tomintoul.

By 1858 George and his son John Gordon Smith had built a much larger distillery at Minmore and closed down both Delnabo and Upper Drumin. The new distillery had a capacity of 600 gallons a week. As a result of the energy of their agent Andrew Usher, the production was soon heavily in demand and in 1864 being exported abroad. In 1871 John Gordon Smith inherited the distillery on his father's death. In 1880 he established by due process of law that no one else was legally entitled to the use of the name The Glenlivet, but all others must use a prefix. John Gordon Smith was succeeded in 1901 by his nephew George Smith Grant, son of Captain William Grant of Auchorachan.

In 1921 the distillery went to Captain W. H. Smith Grant, his younger son. In 1952 George and J. G. Smith Ltd merged with J. & J. Grant, Glen Grant Distillery, forming the Glenlivet and Glen Grant Distilleries Ltd. In 1970 they merged yet again with the noted blender Hill Thomson & Co. Ltd and Longmorn-Glenlivet Distilleries Ltd, when the name of the merged companies was rationalised to The Glenlivet Distillers Ltd. In 1978 their long record of independence came to an end with their acquisition by Seagram Distillers plc.

OWNED BY
Seagram Distillers plc

VISITORS
Reception centre. Tel: 01542 783220

AGE AND STRENGTH WHEN BOTTLED
12 years at 40% volume

COMMENTS
There is an understandable, if deplorable, tendency for Seagram Distillers to reduce the independence and long-standing reputation of the product of this company to just one item in their extensive, if notable, drinks portfolio. Although still an excellent and outstanding malt whisky, there is perhaps already a suspicion of a blander style becoming more apparent than in the past. They should leave well enough alone.

Glenlossie

Situation

Elgin, Morayshire. Grampian Region

Classification

Highland (Speyside)

Origins and Background

This distillery was built in 1876 at Thomshill, about 3 miles south of Elgin. It was founded by a syndicate of three formed by a local hotel owner, John Duff. When the partnership changed in 1896 it was agreed to form The Glenlossie-Glenlivet Distillery Co. Ltd. Considerable development throughout the following months, including a private railway line to Longmorn Station and a new warehouse, resulted in the company going public in 1897. The effects of the recession in the Scotch whisky industry during the ensuing years, however, resulted in the Scottish Malt Distillers Ltd taking them over in 1919. In 1930 the company was dissolved and the distillery became part of Scottish Malt Distillers Ltd. The bulk still goes for blending, but some is now available.

Owned By

United Distillers plc

Visitors

No

Age and Strength When Bottled

10 years at 43% volume

Comments

Although not widely available, this does seem to make a pleasant dram well worth bottling and a welcome addition to the available single malts.

GLENMORANGIE *(glen morange-y)*

SITUATION
Tain, Ross-shire. Highland Region

CLASSIFICATION
Highland (Northern)

ORIGINS AND BACKGROUND
Overlooking the Dornoch Firth near the town of Tain, it is claimed that brewing and distilling has been carried on at or around this site since the Middle Ages. The present distillery, however, only dates from 1843, when William Matheson and his brother converted the brewery operating there into a distillery. Its name derives from the Morangie Burn, which runs through a small glen beside it. It obtains water from a spring rich in minerals from which the brewers who preceded them had taken water for their ale, then renowned as far south as Inverness. In 1893 a private siding connected the distillery to the main railway line, which not only improved the transport of whisky to the south, but also made it easier to obtain supplies of local peat, until these were exhausted. It was here that the use of steam coils in the stills to separate the alcohol from the wash to avoid affecting the whisky's flavour was initiated and subsequently copied by a number of others in the Highlands. In 1918 the distillery was acquired by Macdonald & Muir Ltd and now produces about 600,000 gallons a year, mostly bottled at 10 years.

OWNED BY
Macdonald Martin Distilleries plc

VISITORS
Reception centre. Tel: 01862 892043

AGE AND STRENGTH WHEN BOTTLED
10 years at 40% and 18 years at 43% volume

COMMENTS
A distinctive and very smooth predinner dram that is also mellow enough to be drunk with pleasure after a meal. Well known and deservedly well liked.

GLENORDIE OR ORD: *see* GLEN ORD

GLENROTHES

SITUATION
Rothes, Morayshire. Grampian Region

CLASSIFICATION
Highland (Speyside)

ORIGINS AND BACKGROUND
The distillery was built on the site of an old sawmill in 1878 by a syndicate of Rothes and Elgin businessmen. It went into production in 1879 and eight years later in 1887 merged with the Islay Distillery Co. to form the Highland Distillers Co. Ltd. Since then there has been periodic extensive renovation and rebuilding. A comparatively recently completed still-house has two new pairs of stills, giving a capacity overall of around 5.3 million litres of spirit. Although much still goes for blending, this is now also bottled at 12 and 15 years old and is found in various outlets.

OWNED BY
The Highland Distilleries Co. plc

VISITORS
Reception centre. Tel: 01340 831248

AGE AND STRENGTH WHEN BOTTLED
12 and 15 years old at 43%

COMMENTS
The 12-year-old is a good smooth dram with a pleasing aftermath and well worth bottling. The 15-year-old is sold in a round bottle as Glenrothes Vintage.

Glentauchers

Situation

Mulben, Banffshire. Grampian Region

Classification

Highland (Speyside)

Origins and Background

This distillery was built by James Buchanan, promoter of the famed Black and White blend and prominent amongst the Big Five of the late-19th-century whisky boom. Although primarily a skilful salesman and promoter of blended whiskies, he naturally became involved in the power struggle between the grain whisky and the pot-still malt whisky distillers. However, he decided in 1898 that he needed his own supplies of malt whisky and built this distillery at Glentauchers in association with his Glaswegian whisky broker, W. P. Lowrie. The controlling company was named the Glentauchers-Glenlivet Distillery Co. Ltd, which in 1906, on W. P. Lowrie's retirement, was taken over by James Buchanan & Co. Ltd. In due course, in 1925 the distillery became part of the DCL empire. The malt whisky has from time to time been bottled at 5 and 12 years old, but is now only available from the independent bottlers. Mostly used for blending, it was closed in 1985 but since its acquisition by Allied Distillers in 1989, is to be reopened.

Owned by

Allied Distillers Ltd

Visitors

By arrangement

Age and Strength when Bottled

Only bottled by the independent bottlers

Comments

A 20-year-old at 46% volume seemed to be a very light and dry predinner malt but possibly too long in the cask. It will be interesting to taste this from the distillery again in the late 1990s.

Glenturret

Situation

Crieff, Perthshire. Highland Region

Classification

Highland (Southern)

Origins and Background

Glenturret claims to be the oldest distillery in Scotland, established in 1775, when illicit distilling was widespread. It is well placed between two hills on the banks of the Turret water, providing a good water supply. Over the years it had a succession of proprietors, prominent amongst whom was a Crieff landowner, Thomas Stewart. In 1959 Mr James Fairlie took over as managing director and distiller and a steady programme of renovation and rebulding began. Although small, with a capacity of 400,000 litres, in 1974 the distillery was awarded a Gold Medal in the International Wine and Spirit Competition, repeating this feat in 1981 and again in 1991, along with numerous other recent international prizes under the direction of James Fairlie's son Peter and with third-generation still-man Charlie Brock. In 1981 Glenturret Distillery Ltd was taken over by Cointreau SA, the French liqueur makers, and in 1990 acquired from them by Highland Distilleries, Co. plc. It has since gone from strength to strength, proving the merits of continuity in management and workforce in the distilling of malt whisky. Geared to tourism it is open throughout the year.

Owned By

Highland Distilleries Co. plc

Visitors

Restaurant and reception centre. Tel: 01764 656565

Age and Strength When Bottled

12, 15, 18, and 21 years at 40% volume

Comments

This is an unusual, very late maturing but sound malt whisky with a full smooth flavour and good aftermath suitable for an after-dinner dram.

Highland Park

Situation
Kirkwall, Orkney

Classification
Island (Orkney)

Origins and Background
The distillery is built on a hill overlooking Kirkwall on the site of the bothy of an illicit distiller named Magnus Eunson, who started distilling there in the 18th century. He was an unprincipled rogue who took advantage of his position as church officer to evade capture of his illicit whisky by hiding it under the pulpit. The early history of the distillery is vague, but it is said to have been started legally by David Robertson around 1789. In 1888 James Grant, whose father had been the chief distiller and manager of the Glenlivet Distillery, became managing partner and in 1895 he acquired full control. The Grant family retained control until 1937, when the distillery was acquired by Highland Distilleries Ltd. The distillery has its own maltings although barley has to be imported from the mainland. The water supply comes from two local wells. The Orkney peat used has a distinctive aroma and a small quantity of heather is burnt with it, which may account for the distinctive flavour of this very fine malt whisky from the most northerly distillery in Scotland.

Owned By
Highland Distilleries Co. plc

Visitors
Reception centre. Tel: 01856 873107

Age and Strength When Bottled
12 years at 40% volume

Comments
This has to be acknowledged as one of the finest after-dinner drams. It is smooth and full of character with a fine aftermath and, although recently altered, the distinctively shaped bottle is still a welcome sight.

IMPERIAL

SITUATION
Carron, Morayshire. Grampian Region

CLASSIFICATION
Highland (Speyside)

ORIGINS AND BACKGROUND
The distillery was established in 1887 by Thomas Mackenzie, who already owned Dailuaine and the Talisker Distilleries. He incorporated all three distilleries in 1898 as the Dailuaine-Talisker Distilleries Ltd. In 1916 the company was acquired jointly by Dewar, DCL, W. P. Lowrie, and Johnnie Walker, thus ending up as part of the DCL in 1925, the year of the great mergers into DCL. The product all went for blending, except for some bottled independently. Acquired in 1989 by Allied Distillers Ltd.

OWNED BY
Allied Distillers Ltd

VISITORS
By arrangement

AGE AND STRENGTH WHEN BOTTLED
Only bottled by the independent bottlers

COMMENTS
On one sample this seems to be well worth bottling as an interesting after-dinner dram.

INCHGOWER

SITUATION
Buckie, Banffshire. Grampian Region

CLASSIFICATION
Highland (Speyside)

ORIGINS AND BACKGROUND
Originally established in 1824 as Tochineal Distillery close to Cullen by Alexander Wilson, the distillery was moved in 1871 by Alexander Wilson & Co. to Rathven, a small village about one and a half miles east of Buckie, to ensure a ready supply of water from the Letter Burn and the springs at Aultmoor. In 1933 it was acquired and run by Buckie Town Council, but its period of municipal ownership ended when it was acquired by A. K. Bell in 1936 on behalf of Arthur Bell & Sons, now themselves acquired by Guinness plc, and merged with DCL as United Distilleries plc.

OWNED BY
United Distillers plc

VISITORS
No

AGE AND STRENGTH WHEN BOTTLED
14 years at 43% volume

COMMENTS
A medium-light malt with a touch of sweetness, making a pleasant distinctive dram.

KININVIE

SITUATION

Dufftown, Banffshire. Grampian Region

CLASSIFICATION

Highland (Speyside)

ORIGINS AND BACKGROUND

Another distillery to add to the two already built over the years by William Grant & Sons at Dufftown. The Kininvie Distillery is named after the nearby Kininvie Estate and is situated about 500 yards from the well-known Glenfiddich distillery. This modern plant was planned in the 1980s and takes its water from the same Robbie Dubh spring as Glenfiddich. It came on-stream in July 1990 and has two wash-stills with a capacity of 10,600 litres and four spirit-stills with a capacity of 6,900 litres, rather larger than Glenfiddich itself.

OWNED BY

William Grant & Sons, Ltd

VISITORS

No

AGE AND STRENGTH WHEN BOTTLED

None as yet bottled

COMMENTS

So far it is only for blending and none is bottled as a single malt, but in six or eight years a new single malt may well appear on the market. It will be interesting then to compare it with Glenfiddich, since both distilleries obtain their water from the same source, the Robbie Dubh spring.

KNOCKANDO

SITUATION

Knockando, Morayshire. Grampian Region

CLASSIFICATION

Highland (Speyside)

ORIGINS AND BACKGROUND

The distillery was built by Ian Thompson at the end of the whisky boom and only went into small-scale production for a couple of years before closing down and falling into disrepair, but in 1904 it was bought cheaply by W. & A. Gilbey. The Gaelic meaning of the name is "black hill" and it is in a good position above the Spey with a good water supply. The distillery has a capacity of 750,000 gallons and is now owned by International Distillers & Vintners. While most of the production goes into the well-known J & B Rare Blend, this is the best known of the IDV malt whiskies.

OWNED BY

International Distillers & Vintners Ltd

VISITORS

By arrangement only. Tel: 01340 810205

AGE AND STRENGTH WHEN BOTTLED

Generally from around 13 to 15 years at 40% and 43% volume

COMMENTS

This is a light and smooth after-dinner dram with a good distinctive aftermath. It is a pleasing Speyside malt whisky, bottled when considered at its best by the distillery manager. The dates of distilling and bottling are on the label.

Knockdhu *(nok-doo)*

Situation
Knock, Banffshire. Grampian Region

Classification
Highland (Speyside)

Origins and Background
Knockdhu stands above the small river Isla, from which it draws its water. It was built in 1893 and is of historic interest in that it was the first malt whisky distillery to be built by the DCL. All its production was used for blending, but some was occasionally available as a malt whisky from the independent bottlers. The distillery was closed in 1983 during the recession in the industry, but it is a sign of the times that it was acquired in 1988 by Inver House Distillers Ltd, and restarted distilling in 1989. It is now sold under the name An Cnoc, the Gaelic for Knockdhu.

Owned by
Inver House Distillers Ltd

Visitors
Welcome. Tel: 01466 771223

Age and Strength when Bottled
12 years at 40% volume

Comments
This is a medium-dry after-dinner dram with a pleasing aftermath.

Lagavulin *(lag-avoolin)*

Situation

Port Ellen, Islay, Argyll. Strathclyde Region

Classification

Islay (Island West Coast)

Origins and Background

The Gaelic meaning of Lagavulin is "the mill in the valley" and the distillery claims to date as far back as 1742, but the modern distillery was probably built nearer 1824. It is built close beside the village of Lagavulin in a small bay with its own jetty and obtains its water from the lochs in the hill of Solan. There were a number of owners in the 19th century, but the Grahams went into partnership with James Logan Mackie, uncle of the famous Peter Mackie, who was to become prominent amongst the Big Five in the late 19th century. It was at Lagavulin that Peter Mackie learned his craft as a distiller, and on his uncle's death in the late 1880s he inherited the distillery. The whisky was used as the basis for his famous White Horse blend on which his subsequent reputation was founded. When DCL took over Mackie & Co., Distillers, Ltd., after his death in 1927, they changed the name to White Horse Distillers Ltd, one of the few examples of a company being named after a blend rather than vice versa. The bulk of the production still goes for blending but it is now readily available.

Owned By

United Distillers plc

Visitors

Reception centre. Tel: 01496 302400

Age and Strength When Bottled

16 years at 43% volume

Comments

A full-bodied malt whisky with a powerful iodine flavour and aftermath, it has all the distinctive Islay character. Considered by many to be the most distinctive of the Islay malt whiskies, it has a notable smoothness, making a memorable dram. Another of the Classic Malts.

Laphroaig *(la-froig)*

SITUATION

Port Ellen, Islay, Argyll. Strathclyde Region

CLASSIFICATION

Islay (Island West Coast)

ORIGINS AND BACKGROUND

About 1 mile from Port Ellen, this distillery is in a most attractive position set on a small bay protected by rocky islets. It was built around 1820, operated illicitly by two brothers, Donald and Alexander Johnston. Donald Johnston took over sole control in 1836, by which time the distillery was licensed and legal. Ownership passed through the family until in 1928 Ian Hunter became sole owner. In 1950 he formed a private limited company, D. Johnston & Co. Ltd, with a Miss E. L. Williamson (later Mrs Campbell) as secretary and director. On his death in 1954 she took over his post of managing director. When the company was acquired by Long John International Ltd, acting for Seager Evans & Co., in 1967, she continued as chairman and director until her death in 1972, a rare example of a female in charge of what is largely a male preserve. Much of the whisky goes to make the notable blend Islay Mist, but fortunately some is bottled by the distillery, now acquired by Allied Distillers Ltd.

OWNED BY

Allied Distillers Ltd

VISITORS

Welcome by appointment. Tel: 01496 302418

AGE AND STRENGTH WHEN BOTTLED

10 and 15 years at 40% volume

COMMENTS

A very distinctive Islay dram, slightly sweeter and not as full bodied as Lagavulin, but possibly none the worse for that. The 15-year-old is drier and more full bodied, but at either age like Lagavulin this is a malt whisky about which strong views are held both for and against.

Ledaig: *see* TOBERMORY

Linkwood

SITUATION
Elgin, Morayshire. Grampian Region

CLASSIFICATION
Highland (Speyside)

ORIGINS AND BACKGROUND
Standing just a mile outside Elgin in wooded surroundings, this distillery was originally established by Peter Brown in 1821. It was named after the old mansion house that it replaced. The distillery was largely rebuilt by his son William Brown in 1873. Control was passed to the Linkwood-Glenlivet Distillery Ltd in 1896. For 30 years from 1902, until 1932, the company was managed by a Mr Innes Cameron, who established its reputation as producing a sound malt whisky. On his death the distillery was acquired by the DCL. It is still produced as a malt whisky, although much goes for blending.

OWNED BY
United Distillers plc

VISITORS
No

AGE AND STRENGTH WHEN BOTTLED
12 years at 40% volume

COMMENTS
A very much underrated malt whisky, this is a very good, slightly peaty and very clean-tasting Speyside dram with a good aftermath well worth drinking at any time.

Littlemill

Situation

Bowling, Dunbartonshire. Strathclyde Region

Classification

Lowland (Western)

Origins and Background

Possibly amongst the oldest distilleries in Scotland, its exact origins are uncertain. It is thought that as far back as 1750 a Glasgow maltster, George Buchanan, purchased the estate of Auchterlonie, which included the site of Littlemill. When distilling as opposed to brewing started it is impossible to say. The probability is that the present distillery dates from around 1800, but there were numerous owners until a Duncan G. Thomas, a US citizen, took it over in 1931 and formed the Littlemill Distillery Co. Ltd. In 1959 Barton Brands Inc. of Chicago became shareholders and in 1971 bought out D. G. Thomas and took over control, forming Barton Distilling (Scotland) Ltd. Following a management buyout in 1988, Barton International became Gibson International and control passed to the Loch Lomond Distillery Co. Ltd. Since it uses Highland peat and water from the Kilpatrick hills, this might be regarded as a borderline case, but it is rightly classified as Lowland. Most of the whisky was used for blending, but some was bottled by the distillery, which is now closed.

Owned by

Loch Lomond Distillery Co. Ltd

Visitors

No

Age and Strength when Bottled

8 years at 40% volume

Comments

A light and rather pleasing, smooth predinner dram. It was bottled at 5 and 8 years but the 8-year-old was very much superior and the 5-year-old was quickly discontinued.

Loch Lomond

Situation

Alexandria. Strathclyde Region

Classification

Highland (Southwestern)

Origins and Background

Located at Alexandria, close to Loch Lomond, from which it takes its name, the distillery was built on the site of an old printing and bleach works. It was also built almost exactly on the imaginary Highland Line and just qualifies as producing a Highland malt whisky. The stills are unusual in that incorporated with them is a rectifying head, which can be altered to produce different weights of whisky. The bulk of the malt whisky produced goes for blending. After the takeover of Barton Distilling (Scotland) Ltd by Amalgamated Distilled Products plc in 1982, control passed to the Loch Lomond Distiller Co. Ltd. Some malt whisky is now distilled and bottled under the name Inchmurrin after a prominent island on nearby Loch Lomond. Using the rectifying head on the same stills, a separate malt whisky named Rossdhu, after a sandbank above the island, is also distilled. A grain distillery has been added.

Owned By

Loch Lomond Distillery Co. Ltd

Visitors

By arrangement

Age and Strength When Bottled

Inchmurrin at 10 years at 40% volume, Rossdhu unaged at 43% volume

Comments

Somewhat hard to find, Inchmurrin is an interesting if rather light single malt. Rossdhu is even lighter, but the age gap makes judging difficult.

Lochnager: *see* Royal Lochnagar

Lochside

Situation
Lochside, Montrose, Angus. Grampian Region

Classification
Highland (Eastern)

Origins and Background
Built originally in the 18th century as a brewery, which it still resembles, the actual date when it was established and the names of its early owners have been forgotten. In the early 19th century it was owned by a William Ross, who sold it to James Deuchar & Sons Ltd of Newcastle on Tyne. It was later bought by Scottish & Newcastle Breweries Ltd, who shipped the beer from Montrose to Newcastle. Finally, in 1957, it was acquired by Joseph W. Hobbs, who already owned the Ben Nevis distillery, and was converted into a distillery capable, like Ben Nevis, of producing grain and malt whisky with a patent-still alongside the pot malt stills. The company in whose name it was controlled was MacNab Distilleries Ltd. In 1973 the large Spanish company Destilerias y Crianza del Whisky S. A. of Madrid, known as DYC for short, acquired the distillery, the first continental takeover of a distillery. They closed down the grain distillery and concentrated on producing Highland malt whisky. The distillery has a capacity of a million proof gallons a year. Most of the production goes for blending in Scotland, although some goes to Italy and some to Spain for use in blended Spanish whisky and some to the independent bottlers. It is now closed.

Owned By
Destilerias y Crianza del Whisky S. A., Madrid (DYC)

Visitors
By arrangement. Tel: 01674 672737

AGE AND STRENGTH WHEN BOTTLED

10 years old at 40% volume

COMMENTS

This seems a smooth enough dry dram. It is to be hoped the distillery will find a new owner.

LOMOND

SITUATION
Dumbarton. Strathclyde Region

CLASSIFICATION
Lowland (Northern)

ORIGINS AND BACKGROUND
In effect this is part of the Inverleven distillery since it uses a unique type of flat-sided still invented by a Hiram Walker employee, now dead, a Mr Fred Whiting. It takes the same low wines and feints charger and the same spirit receiver as Inverleven but the stills produce a whisky quite distinct from the other, thus giving Hiram Walker the advantage of having two separate malts from what is in essence the same distillery complex. The malt whisky produced was all used for blending. Along with Inverleven, it was acquired by Allied Distillers in 1988 and closed in 1992.

OWNED BY
Allied Distillers Ltd

VISITORS
No

AGE AND STRENGTH WHEN BOTTLED
None bottled

COMMENTS
It would have been interesting to be able to test the difference between this and Inverleven for oneself rather than relying on hearsay.

Longmorn

Situation
Elgin, Morayshire. Grampian Region

Classification
Highland (Speyside)

Origins and Background
Two and a half miles south of Elgin near the village of Longmorn, with a water supply from a never-failing local spring and peat obtained from nearby Mannoch Hill, this distillery was built in 1897 by John Duff at the height of the whisky boom. In the same year he also built the neighbouring Benriach distillery. (*See* **Benriach.**) The controlling company was John Duff & Co. Ltd, but in 1898 James R. Grant took over Longmorn, to be succeeded by his sons P. J. C. Grant and R. L. Grant, trading as the Longmorn Distillery Co. The Grants of Longmorn and the Grants of Glen Grant were finally united in 1970 when Hill Thomson & Co. Ltd, noted whisky blenders and merchants of 45 Frederick Street, Edinburgh, where they had been trading since 1799, and Longmorn-Glenlivet Distillers Ltd merged with The Glenlivet and Glen Grant Distilleries Ltd, under the banner of The Glenlivet Distillers. (*See* **The Glenlivet.**) Only eight years later, in 1978, they were acquired by Seagram Distillers plc, thus ending a proud record of independent and dedicated Scottish control.

Owned By
Seagram Distillers plc

Visitors
By arrangement. Tel: 01542 787471

Age and Strength When Bottled
15 years at 45% volume

Comments
This used to be one of the very finest malt whiskies when bottled at 10 years and 40% volume, a fine, very pale and delicate flavour, making it an excellent dram before or

after dinner. After being taken over by Seagram it ceased to be bottled except for the French market. Happily it is now bottled again, but at 15 years, no doubt to fit in with Seagram's marketing policy of having different malts available covering a range of ages. It is now rather darker coloured and with the delicacy and fragrance it formerly had perhaps slightly masked by being too long in the cask. It is still, however, a very fine dram to drink at any time, if you can find it.

LONGROW: *see* SPRINGBANK

MACALLAN

SITUATION
Craigellachie, Banffshire. Grampian Region

CLASSIFICATION
Highland (Speyside)

ORIGINS AND BACKGROUND
The distillery was first licensed legally on the Macallans' farm above a well-known ford over the River Spey and the famous rock of Craigellachie in 1824, but there can be little doubt that illicit distilling had been carried on there for a number of years previously. This was a natural crossing on the Spey for the travelling cattle drovers, who would generally spend a night at the farm, where it was reasonable that they would drink quantities of illicitly distilled whisky. They were also the obvious middle-men between the merchants in the south and the illicit distillers in the north, hence the Macallan farm was ideally placed for illicit distilling. As with The Glenlivet, the reputation of the whisky was already too widespread immediately after the legal licensing of the distillery to account for its popularity in the south in any other way. The Macallan, like The Glenlivet, was off to a head start when the 1823 Act came into being in 1824. Nevertheless, the distillery changed hands several times in the course of the 19th century before James Stuart sold it to Roderick Kemp in 1892. Kemp had been trained as a distiller at Talisker and soon began to improve Macallan.

By the time Kemp died in 1909, Macallan was already regarded as one of the finest Speyside malts. On his death a trust was formed for his two married daughters and their progeny, and their descendants are still prominent shareholders to this day. In 1950 a steady programme of modernisation and rebuilding was introduced over a six-year period, throughout which the distillery continued in full production. In 1959 further rebuilding work was carried out. Finally, in 1964, a second distillery was built alongside the old one and came into production in 1966 as an integral unit with the old.

Production is now around the 1½-million-gallon mark a year, but remains in very high demand as one of the outstanding Highland malts. It may be because of the distillery's insistence on the use of small stills similar to the originals and never using caramel for colouring, but always maturing the spirit in sherry casks. Achieving a standard colouring by blending whiskies from different casks is amongst the secrets of their outstanding success. Certainly this is a classic case where Scottish distillers, unhampered by transatlantic takeovers, or accounting methods, or love of standardisation and modern marketing theories, have proved themselves infinitely superior by using to the full the old methods and the well tried and tested principles of pot-still malt whisky distilling. The malt whisky is marketed as The Macallan.

OWNED BY

The Macallan Distillers Ltd

VISITORS

Reception centre. Tel: 01340 871471

AGE AND STRENGTH WHEN BOTTLED

10 years old at 40% volume; also 12 and 18 years at 43% volume, and 25 years at 43% volume

COMMENTS

If only the success of this fine malt whisky could be a lesson to those transatlantic or foreign conglomerates who now own other fine malt distilleries. In any shape and form The Macallan is a joy to drink, with an initial sweetness but smooth body and splendid aftermath, and it can only be said that as it ages it improves. It is well marketed and deservedly popular.

MACDUFF

SITUATION
Banff, Banffshire. Grampian Region

CLASSIFICATION
Highland (Speyside)

ORIGINS AND BACKGROUND
This distillery is of comparatively recent construction, having been built near Banff in 1962 by a group including Brodie Hepburn Ltd, and Block, Grey and Block Ltd, and drawing its water for cooling from the nearby River Deveron. The original William Lawson was a Dundonian who started business as a whisky merchant and blender from 1849, but his company was never of any great consequence and remained quiescent for a lengthy period. The company was revived after the 1939–45 War in Liverpool as blenders and exporters and in 1967 was moved to Coatbridge, where a bottling and blending unit was formed. In 1980 they became part of the General Beverage Corporation of Luxembourg, themselves a subsidiary company of Martini Rossi. They then bought the 10-year-old Macduff distillery and extended the warehouses. Capacity is now around 750,000 proof gallons. The malt whisky produced is called **Glen Deveron** and is readily available and well marketed.

OWNED BY
General Beverage Corporation, Luxembourg

VISITORS
No. Tel: 01261 812612

AGE AND STRENGTH WHEN BOTTLED
12 years at 40% volume

COMMENTS
A good, straightforward Speyside after-dinner malt whisky, clean tasting with a dry and pleasing aftermath.

MANNOCHMORE

SITUATION

Elgin, Morayshire. Grampian Region

CLASSIFICATION

Highland (Speyside)

ORIGINS AND BACKGROUND

This distillery was built by John Haig & Co. Ltd in 1971 about 2½ miles south of Elgin, alongside their malt distillery at Glenlossie, but drawing its water from another source. It has a capacity of a million proof gallons, but most of the production goes for blending.

OWNED BY

United Distillers plc

VISITORS

No

AGE AND STRENGTH WHEN BOTTLED

12 years at 43% volume

COMMENTS

Like neighbouring Glenlossie, not widely available but a welcome addition to the range of single malts on the market. United Distillers is to be congratulated on reversing the old die-hard attitudes of the DCL to bottling and marketing them.

Miltonduff

Situation
Elgin, Morayshire. Grampian Region

Classification
Highland (Speyside)

Origins and Background
Close to the famed Pluscarden Abbey ruins, this distillery was built in 1824 in the year when the 1823 Licensing Act came into force. It is almost certain, therefore, that it was built on the site of a previously illicit distillery and its mash house is said to have been built on the old abbey brewhouse. The water from the Black Burn flowing from the peaty slopes of the Black Hill provides an ample water supply. It was established by Messrs Bain and Pearey, but was soon transferred to William Stuart. During the early 1890s a good deal of renovation and rebuilding took place, and by 1896 it was capable of producing 300,000 proof gallons a year. After the whisky boom, in common with all other malt distilleries, it went through a long lean period. In 1936 Thomas Yool, then owner, sold the distillery to Hiram Walker-Gooderham & Worts, Ltd. It was subsequently modernised and enlarged so that it now has a capacity of 2 million proof gallons a year of over 5 million litres of alcohol. At one period another malt whisky known as **Mosstowie** was also produced from this complex, in Lomond-type stills (*see* **Loch Lomond**) but these have now been dismantled, although some of the product may still be available through the independent bottlers.

Owned By
Allied Distillers Ltd

Visitors
Reception centre. Tel: 01343 547433

Age and Strength When Bottled
12 years at 43% volume

Comments
A very reasonable Speyside after-dinner malt whisky, smooth and with a delicate aftermath.

MORTLACH

SITUATION
Dufftown, Banffshire. Grampian Region

CLASSIFICATION
Highland (Speyside)

ORIGINS AND BACKGROUND
This distillery owes its name to the parish in which it lies. The Gaelic meaning of Mortlach is "a bowl-shaped valley" and the distillery stands in a hollow in the hills just outside Dufftown on the River Dullan, but draws its water from a locally famed Priests' well. Although undoubtedly based on the site of an earlier illicit still, it was first licensed in 1824 to John Findlater. In the following year he took on two partners, Gordon and Mackintosh. By 1854 Gordon was the sole survivor and was joined in that year by George Cowie. Ten years later, in 1865, George Cowie was the sole owner. Trading as George Cowie & Sons, the company apparently benefitted from the whisky boom and was thoroughly rebuilt and renovated in 1903. After surviving the recession during the 1914–18 War, it was acquired by John Walker & Sons Ltd, in 1923, thus becoming part of the DCL and now part of United Distillers plc.

OWNED BY
United Distillers plc

VISITORS
No

AGE AND STRENGTH WHEN BOTTLED
12 years old and 40% volume

COMMENTS
A mellow Speyside malt whisky making a very pleasing after-dinner dram with a good aftermath.

MOSSTOWIE: *see* MILTONDUFF

OBAN

SITUATION
Oban, Argyll. Strathclyde Region

CLASSIFICATION
Highland (Western)

ORIGINS AND BACKGROUND
It is claimed by some that Oban is the oldest distillery to have been in continuous production. It is said that distilling began in 1794, since when it has had a number of owners. In 1883 it was acquired by James Walter Higgins. Then in 1898 it was bought by the Oban and Aultmore Distilleries Ltd with the intention of acting as a major supplier to the notorious Pattison Ltd, of Leith, whose bankruptcy in that year signalled the end of the whisky boom. It was indicative of the distillery's strength that it survived their failure and was only sold again in 1923, when a partnership bought it and formed the Oban Distillery Co. Ltd. In 1930 the Scottish Malt Distillers Ltd acquired the company and it became part of the DCL. It was closed in 1968, but was opened again in 1969, barely spoiling its claim for continuous operation.

OWNED BY
United Distillers plc

VISITORS
Reception centre. Tel: 01631 564262

AGE AND STRENGTH WHEN BOTTLED
14 years at 43% volume

COMMENTS
This is a very pleasing, distinctive malt whisky with plenty of body and a good aftermath, possibly a little more like a Highland than West Coast dram, but equally suitable for drinking before or after dinner. Another Classic Malt.

OLD FETTERCAIRN: *see* FETTERCAIRN

OLD PULTENEY: *see* PULTENEY

PITTYVAICH

SITUATION
Dufftown, Banffshire. Grampian Region

CLASSIFICATION
Highland (Speyside)

ORIGINS AND BACKGROUND
This was built in 1974 on the outskirts of Dufftown in the Dullan Glen by Arthur Bell & Sons Ltd, close to their other distillery, named after the town. The water for the distillery is drawn from two springs, Balliemore and Convalleys. It has four stills, which are exact replicas of those in its older neighbour, and it operates in conjunction with the latter as part of the same distillery complex. The entire production goes for blending and is not bottled separately. The distillery sometimes uses the Glenlivet affix, for which there is surely no justification. It is now part of the United Distillers plc, but is currently closed.

OWNED BY
United Distillers plc

VISITORS
No

AGE AND STRENGTH WHEN BOTTLED
12 years at 43% volume

COMMENTS
A little is bottled but it is not commercially available.

PULTENEY

SITUATION

Wick, Caithness. Highland Region

CLASSIFICATION

Highland (Northernmost)

ORIGINS AND BACKGROUND

Established in 1826, near the town of Wick, the distillery is not far from that notable landmark above the town, the ruined castle on the cliffs known as the Auld Man of Wick. There are ample water supplies available, including the Loch of Hempriggs. Peat, of course, is no problem in a countryside where houses were frequently roofed with it. The lack of good road and rail communication is, however, indicated by the fact that this is the only distillery in Caithness and the most northerly on the mainland. The distillery remained under control of the Henderson family until the slump of the 1920s, when in 1923 it was acquired by James Watson & Co. Ltd. Like many other malt distilleries, it was then closed down in 1926 during the depression years and remained closed for a long period, until 1951. By then it had been acquired by Mr R. Cumming and it was bought from him in turn by Hiram Walker & Sons (Scotland) plc. They licensed it to their subsidiary J. & G. Stodart Ltd, and set about extensive renovation and modernisation. The bulk of their whisky goes for blending. Acquired by Inver House Distillers in 1995. It is bottled as **Old Pulteney,** but see below.

OWNED BY

Inver House Distillers

VISITORS

Reception centre. Tel: 01955 602371

AGE AND STRENGTH WHEN BOTTLED

8 years old at 40% volume

COMMENTS

This is amongst the fastest maturing of the Highland malt whiskies. It is indeed light, clean, and smooth and a good predinner dram, but hardly merits the prefix Old.

ROSEBANK

SITUATION

Camelon, Falkirk, Stirlingshire. Central Region

CLASSIFICATION

Lowland

ORIGINS AND BACKGROUND

According to the Statistical Account for Scotland of the period, Messrs Stark Brothers were distilling here in 1798, but the forerunner of the present distillery complex was begun by James Rankine in 1840 and the site was originally chosen for its ready water supplies. In 1864 he was followed by his son R. W. Rankine, who rebuilt the entire distillery and increased demand for the distillery's product greatly. In 1894 the Rosebank Distillery Ltd was formed as a public company and a second issue of shares in 1897 was immediately fully subscribed. With the collapse of the whisky boom in 1900 and the slump that followed, however, Rosebank was badly hit and in 1914 was one of the companies that amalgamated to form Scottish Malt Distillers Ltd, becoming a subsidiary of the DCL and now of United Distillers plc. It was closed in 1993.

OWNED BY

United Distillers plc

VISITORS

No

AGE AND STRENGTH WHEN BOTTLED

12 years at 43% volume

COMMENTS

A dry dram with a good flavour and plenty of body, it tastes more like a Highland than the Lowland malt whisky it undoubtedly is. It is no longer commercially available.

ROYAL BRACKLA

SITUATION
Nairn, Morayshire. Grampian Region

CLASSIFICATION
Highland (Northern)

ORIGINS AND BACKGROUND
The distillery was founded at Cawdor, close to Nairn, in 1812 by Captain William Fraser and received the prefix "Royal" in 1835 at the command of William IV to show his approval of the whisky. Whether "Silly Billy"'s commendation was up to much is another matter, but it probably helped to sell the whisky over the years. The distillery changed hands a number of times before the Brackla Distillery Co. Ltd was formed in 1898 and acquired the lease and more land from the Earl of Cawdor for expansion. In 1919 John Mitchell and James Leith of Aberdeen acquired the company and in 1926 sold it to John Bisset & Co. Ltd of Leith. In 1943 they were taken over by DCL. Subsequently, in 1965, the distillery was modernised and expanded with steam-fired stills of 5,000-gallon capacity and a new malting. Almost all the production goes for blending.

OWNED BY
United Distillers plc

VISITORS
No

AGE AND STRENGTH WHEN BOTTLED
10 years old at 43% volume

COMMENTS
An independent bottling at 18 years old and 46% volume made a very good after-dinner dram with plenty of body and pleasing aftermath, which suggests that at 10 years, if a bottle can be found, it should be a worthwhile dram.

ROYAL LOCHNAGAR

SITUATION

Crathie, Ballater, Aberdeenshire. Grampian Region

CLASSIFICATION

Highland (Eastern)

ORIGINS AND BACKGROUND

The Lochnagar distillery, only a mile from Balmoral, was built by John Begg in 1845. In 1848 on 12th September Queen Victoria, accompanied by Prince Albert and her young family, toured the distillery, being personally escorted by John Begg himself, who persuaded them all to try a dram, for which service he duly received a royal warrant. The distillery was known for much of the 19th century as the Royal Lochnagar Distillery. The advertising slogan "Take a peg of John Begg" was one of the earlier examples of the kind. John Begg was a considerable entrepreneur in his day and from Aberdeen initially set up a worldwide export and blending business, finally based in Glasgow. On his death in 1880 his son Henry Begg took over and continued the business as John Begg. In 1916 they were taken over by DCL and the Royal prefix was dropped for some time, but has since been resuscitated. Much of the production goes for blending, but some is bottled as the only example of a Deeside malt whisky.

OWNED BY

United Distillers plc

VISITORS

Reception centre. Tel: 01339 742273

AGE AND STRENGTH WHEN BOTTLED

12 years at 40% volume

COMMENTS

A very pleasant, smooth-tasting, fresh, clean after-dinner dram with a good aftermath.

SCAPA

SITUATION
Kirkwall, Orkney

CLASSIFICATION
Island (Orkney)

ORIGINS AND BACKGROUND
In 1885 Mr J. T. Townsend, a Speyside distiller, built what was then a very advanced distillery 2 miles from Kirkwall, the capital of Orkney, on the north side of Scapa Flow and obtaining its water supplies from the Lingro Burn. It naturally has had very close connections during both world wars, and after the First World War, the German Fleet was scuttled in full view of the distillery. The distillery itself had naval ratings billeted in it during the War and when fire broke out they helped to fight the blaze and save the distillery. After the War, control was passed to the Scapa Distillery Co. Ltd, subsequently taken over by Bloch Brothers (Distillers) Ltd. Then in 1934 Hiram Walker & Sons (Scotland) plc acquired it as part of their plans for venturing into the industry in Scotland, and it was largely rebuilt in 1959. It is licensed to one of their subsidiaries, the blending company Taylor & Ferguson Ltd, also acquired in the 1930s. It is currently shut down.

OWNED BY
Allied Distillers Ltd

VISITORS
By arrangement. Tel: 01856 872071

AGE AND STRENGTH WHEN BOTTLED
It is only obtainable from the independent bottlers.

COMMENTS
A dram at 8 years and 40% volume made a good after-dinner drink recognisable as having a resemblance to the Orkney Highland Park, which makes it sadder that this is not often available.

SINGLETON: *see* AUCHROISK

SINGLETON: *see* AUCHROISK

SPEYBURN

SITUATION
Rothes, Morayshire. Grampian Region

CLASSIFICATION
Highland (Speyside)

ORIGINS AND BACKGROUND
The distillery was built towards the end of the Scotch whisky boom in 1896, by the brothers John and Edward Hopkins in partnership with their cousin Edward Broughton, with whom they controlled the well-known whisky-blending and marketing firm of John Hopkins & Company Ltd, which dated from 1872. There is a plentiful water supply from the springs in the hills of the Glen of Rothes. After building the distillery at Rothes, it was registered in the name of the Speyburn-Glenlivet Distillery Co. Ltd, using the affix Glenlivet. In 1916 John Hopkins was taken over by DCL, but was not totally integrated until 1931. The distillery is not a large one, but it has been prominent in trying to overcome the problem of pollution in the River Spey. The entire production goes for blending and is accepted as of high quality, but a little is occasionally available from the independent bottlers. The distillery was bought from United Distillers by Inver House in 1992.

OWNED BY
Inver House Distillers Ltd

VISITORS
No

AGE AND STRENGTH WHEN BOTTLED
10 years at 40% volume

COMMENTS
A pleasantly mellow Speyside dram that merits drinking at any time.

SPEYSIDE

SITUATION

4 miles south of Kingussie at Drumguish

CLASSIFICATION

Speyside

ORIGINS AND BACKGROUND

In 1958 George P. Christie established the North of Scotland Grain distillery near Cambus, subsequently sold to DCL in 1984. From the 1950s he planned a malt distillery at Drumguish on the site of a 19th-century mill where the River Tromie enters the Spey. The small distillery in local stone built by a single master stonemason, Mr Alexander Fairlie, over 20 years, finally came on-stream in 1990, with stills of half-a-million-gallon capacity. It is a family venture run by George P. Christie's son Roderick George and grandson Nicholas. Currently marketed as Drumguish.

OWNED BY

The Speyside Distillery Co., Ltd

VISITORS

By arrangement. Tel: 0141 353 0110

AGE AND STRENGTH WHEN BOTTLED

Drumguish: unaged at 40% volume

COMMENTS

It is good to see Scots still bucking the trend towards ever larger combines. Drumguish, a good name for a malt, is very young, but it is also fast maturing, and even unaged it makes a smooth and pleasant, typical Speyside dram. At 10 years or over it is planned to be marketed as The Speyside.

SPRINGBANK

SITUATION

Campbeltown, Argyll. Strathclyde Region

CLASSIFICATION

Campbeltown

ORIGINS AND BACKGROUND

Campbeltown was once regarded as the whisky capital of Scotland with something like 40 distilleries in and around the town. Springbank, established by the Mitchell family in the late 1820s, is one of the two remaining and the only one to have survived without closing. It is still owned by J. & A. Mitchell & Co. Ltd, the family concern, the present owners being direct descendants of the founders. An unusual feature is a special spirit-still used for the foreshots and feints instead of returning them for redistillation, as is usual. One other notable feature is that it is one of the few distilleries to bottle its own malt on site. (Another is Glenfiddich.) It should also be noted particularly that the distillery produces two different malt whiskies. As well as Springbank it produces another named Longrow. This is distilled with only peat-dried malted barley, making it much heavier as a result. The distillery has three times won the Championship Award at the Wine & Spirit Fair at Ljubljana in Yugoslavia.

OWNED BY

J. & A. Mitchell & Co. Ltd

VISITORS

By arrangement. Tel: 01586 552085

AGE AND STRENGTH WHEN BOTTLED

12, 15, 21, and 30 years at 46% volume

COMMENTS

Springbank is an interesting and distinctive malt whisky, rather reminiscent of an Irish whiskey with an initial sweetness and a pleasing aftermath, making an altogether very satisfying dram. Longrow at 14 years and 46% is more like a smooth west coast malt whisky, reminiscent of an Islay dram with a long aftermath.

Strathisla

Situation
Keith, Banffshire. Grampian Region

Classification
Highland (Speyside)

Origins and Background
In 1786 a Mr George Taylor obtained a charter from the Earl of Findlater and Seafield for a distillery on the site, thus making this one of the earliest operating distilleries in the Highlands. From around 1830 it was owned and managed by William Longmore and his successors, initially as the Strathisla distillery and latterly as the Milton distillery, a name still used by some locals. It was still a private company when acquired by Chivas Brothers Ltd in 1950, themselves a subsidiary of Seagram Distillers plc, who promptly changed the name back from Milton to Strathisla and added the hyphenated Glenlivet affix, although a considerable distance from the Livet. While still adding the affix to their distillery name, it has now been dropped from the label on the bottle. Strathisla in fact obtain their water supplies for cooling from the River Isla and for distilling from a reservoir filled by a spring in the hills. On the other side of the River Isla stands the sister distillery, Glen Keith (another that used to add the Glenlivet affix), which was built in 1956. Most went for blending but some was bottled by Chivas Brothers and the independent bottlers. It is now widely available.

Owned By
Seagram Distillers plc

Visitors
Reception centre. Tel: 01542 783044

Age and Strength When Bottled
12 years and 43% volume

Comments
Like Glen Keith, this is now readily available and is a pleasantly smooth, medium-bodied, dry after-dinner dram.

STRATHMILL

SITUATION
Keith, Banffshire. Grampian Region

CLASSIFICATION
Highland (Speyside)

ORIGINS AND BACKGROUND
Originally called the Glenisla-Glenlivet Distillery, Strathmill was built on the site of a former mill in 1891 and was acquired by W. & A. Gilbey in 1895 at the height of the Scotch whisky boom. Initially they marketed malt whisky only, but then turned to blending and marketed their noted blend Glen Spey. In 1962 they merged with Gilbey Twiss, Justerini & Brooks, and United Vintners to form the International Distillers & Vintners. The output of the distillery is now all used for blending.

OWNED BY
International Distillers & Vintners Ltd

VISITORS
By arrangement

AGE AND STRENGTH WHEN BOTTLED
None bottled by the distillery

COMMENTS
Some is available from time to time through the independent bottlers.

Talisker

Situation
Carbost, Isle of Skye

Classification
Island (Skye)

Origins and Background
First established in 1830, the distillery was twice moved before settling where it is now sited on the shores of Loch Harport. Its water for distilling is obtained from the nearby Carbost Burn. In 1898 the Talisker Distillery Ltd amalgamated with the Dailuaine-Glenlivet Distillery Ltd, which resulted in the formation of Dailuaine-Talisker Distilleries Ltd, which also controlled the Imperial-Glenlivet Distillery close to Dailuaine. The three distilleries in this group were acquired in 1916 jointly by Dewar, DCL, W. P. Lowrie, and Johnnie Walker. In 1925, at the time of the great amalgamation that saw Dewar and Johnnie Walker both absorbed into DCL, they also became part of DCL and since then have been controlled by Scottish Malt Distillers, although for many years the three were run as a separate company.

Owned By
United Distillers plc

Visitors
Reception centre. Tel: 01478 640203

Age and Strength When Bottled
10 years at 45.8% volume

Comments
A very smooth and pleasing distinctive and unmistakably west coast malt whisky with a full body and strong aftermath, making a notable after-dinner dram. Another of United Distillers' six Classic Malts.

TAMDHU *(tamdoo)*

SITUATION
Knockando, Morayshire. Grampian Region

CLASSIFICATION
Highland (Speyside)

ORIGINS AND BACKGROUND
Yet another of the many distilleries built around the time of the Scotch whisky boom years, this distillery was established in 1897. The Gaelic meaning of Tamdhu is "small black hill" and it is under just such a hill that the distillery lies on the banks of the Spey. In 1898 the controlling company Tamdhu-Glenlivet Ltd was acquired by The Highland Distilleries Co. plc, although operating as a separate subsidiary. In common with many others, the distillery was shut down for a long period, from 1927 to 1948, but, renovated and modernised, it forms an important part of the group. It is now readily available bottled by the distillers.

OWNED BY
The Highland Distilleries Co. plc

VISITORS
Reception centre. Tel: 01340 810221

AGE AND STRENGTH WHEN BOTTLED
Unaged at 40% volume

COMMENTS
A sound, full-bodied malt whisky with a good mellow aftermath, making a pleasing after-dinner dram. It is well marketed and readily obtainable.

TAMNAVULIN-GLENLIVET *(tam-na-voolin)*

SITUATION
Ballindalloch, Banffshire. Grampian Region

CLASSIFICATION
Highland (Speyside)

ORIGINS AND BACKGROUND
The Gaelic meaning of Tamnavulin is "the mill on the hill" and near to the site of this distillery are the ruins of an old mill. It was built by the Invergordon Distillers Ltd in 1966 on the west bank of the River Livet at the base of the Cairngorm mountains. It is among the few distilleries that are entitled to use the hyphenated affix Glenlivet with good reason. Now part of the Whyte & Mackay group since 1993 and currently mothballed.

OWNED BY
Whyte & Mackay Distillers Ltd

VISITORS
No

AGE AND STRENGTH WHEN BOTTLED
10 years at 40% volume

COMMENTS
A light, slightly peaty, typical smooth Speyside malt whisky with a good aftermath, making a pleasing dram at any time.

TEANINICH

SITUATION
Alness, Ross-shire. Highland Region

CLASSIFICATION
Highland (Northern)

ORIGINS AND BACKGROUND
Facing the Cromarty Firth, this distillery probably dates back to the 18th century. Some of the original buildings put up by Captain H. Munro of Teaninich in 1817 are still visible today. The distillery is close to the River Averon, from which its water supplies are obtained. The Teaninich Munros, a branch of the Munros of Foulis, gave up distilling in the 1850s when they let the premises to successive tenants. In 1895 two partners named Munro and Cameron took over the distillery and acquired the lease from the Munro family. In 1905, on his partner's death, Robert Innes Cameron took over the entire operation. In 1933 his trustees sold out to the DCL. The entire production went for blending, but the distillery has only recently reopened after being closed for some years. Some is now bottled.

OWNED BY
United Distillers plc

VISITORS
No

AGE AND STRENGTH WHEN BOTTLED
10 years at 43% volume

COMMENTS
Even if in restricted supply, it is good to have this satisfactory single malt available once again.

TOBERMORY

SITUATION
Tobermory, Mull, Argyll. Highland Region

CLASSIFICATION
Island (Mull)

ORIGINS AND BACKGROUND
The distillery dates back to the start of the 18th century, when there was undoubtedly a good deal of illicit distilling on the island. After its foundation it had a number of owners until bought by John Hopkins & Co. Ltd around 1890. In 1916 the distillery became part of the DCL. It was shut down in 1928 and was used as an electricity-generating station. In 1972 a Liverpool Shipping Company financed a complete rebuilding and re-equipping of the distillery, with assistance from Spanish and Panamanian backers, and formed a company called the Ledaig Distillery (Tobermory) Ltd, and it was then bottled as Ledaig. By 1975 the company closed down, having just raised the distillery's capacity to 800,000 gallons a year. In 1976 a Receiver was appointed, but in 1979 the Kirkleavington Property Co. took over and started operating as the Tobermory Distillers Ltd. The bulk of the production went for blending, but it was also available as a malt whisky. Unfortunately, it closed again in 1981, but distilling started again in 1990 and in 1993 it was acquired by Burn Stewart.

OWNED BY
Burn Stewart Distillers plc

VISITORS
By arrangement

AGE AND STRENGTH WHEN BOTTLED
No age given at 40% volume

COMMENTS
A peaty malt whisky more like a Speyside product than a west coast island dram. It will be interesting to taste it when more mature.

TOMATIN

SITUATION

Tomatin, Inverness-shire. Highland Region

CLASSIFICATION

Highland (Northern)

ORIGINS AND BACKGROUND

About 13 miles southeast of Inverness and built around the 1,028-foot level, this distillery is remote enough, although within easy reach of the main road and the railway. Established in 1897, it survived the succeeding years well and up to the outbreak of the Second World War was eminently successful. On resuming distilling after the War the distillery was producing 120,000 proof gallons from its two pot-stills a year. After successive programmes of modernisation the number of stills was increased to 23, with a capacity of 5 million proof gallons by 1975.

A high degree of automation and the latest methods were introduced throughout the entire distilling process, so that only a small workforce was required, despite the size of operation. Water for the distilling process is obtained from the Monadhliaith Mountains via a local burn, the Alt-na-Frithe, which flows into the River Findhorn not far away. After a series of financial upsets, the company was forced to close the distillery temporarily and was finally acquired in 1986 by the Japanese company Takara Shuzo & Okura, the first whisky distillery to be taken over by Japanese interests. Most goes for blending but it is also exported in bulk. Nevertheless, it is also available as a malt whisky.

OWNED BY

Takara Shuzo & Okura Co. Ltd

VISITORS

Reception centre. Tel: 01808 511234

AGE AND STRENGTH WHEN BOTTLED

10 years at 40% volume

COMMENTS

A medium smooth, fairly bland, predinner dram.

TOMINTOUL–GLENLIVET *(tomin-towl)*

SITUATION
Ballindalloch, Banffshire. Grampian Region

CLASSIFICATION
Highland (Speyside)

ORIGINS AND BACKGROUND
This modern distillery was established in 1965 by two firms of Glasgow whisky brokers, Hay & MacLeod & Co. and W. & S. Strong & Co., because of the shortage of malt whisky available for blending at that time. They chose a site some 5 miles north of Tomintoul close to the Glenlivet area with a plentiful supply of water from the Ballantruan Spring. Later additions brought the total capacity up to a million proof gallons, or 2.52 million litres of alcohol a year, with storage on the spot for 2½ million gallons, or 6.3 million litres of alcohol. The founder firms of whisky brokers subsequently merged with Whyte & Mackay Ltd. Most of the production goes into Whyte & Mackay blends, but some is bottled and the Glenlivet affix is justified.

OWNED BY
Whyte & Mackay Distillers Ltd

VISITORS
Reception centre. Tel: 01807 590274

AGE AND STRENGTH WHEN BOTTLED
12 years at 40% volume

COMMENTS
A very light and smooth predinner dram with a good aftermath.

TORMORE

SITUATION

Advie, Grantown-on-Spey. Grampian Region

CLASSIFICATION

Highland (Speyside)

ORIGINS AND BACKGROUND

Built in 1959 by Seager Evans & Co. Ltd, this was the first completely new distillery to be built on Speyside this century. It was built to a totally new design by a past President of the Royal Academy, Sir Albert Richardson. It was a complete breakaway from traditional designs and consists of a distillery, warehouses, and cooperage, as well as houses for the distillery workers, all built in Kemnay granite. Ample water supplies are available, supposedly from the nearby Loch an Oir, which in Gaelic means Loch of Gold. Much of the product is used for blending but some is bottled for the distillery, now acquired from Long John International Ltd by Allied Distillers Ltd.

OWNED BY

Allied Distillers Ltd

VISITORS

Welcome by arrangement. Tel: 01807 510244

AGE AND STRENGTH WHEN BOTTLED

10 years at 40% volume

COMMENTS

A medium and fairly typical Speyside malt whisky with a pleasant aftermath, making a satisfactory if rather light pre-dinner dram. It is also bottled as a 5-year-old at 43% volume but for export only. This is, however, generally obtainable at airports in the duty-free shops and is also a good dram.

TULLIBARDINE *(tulli-bar-deen)*

SITUATION
Blackford, Perthshire. Highland Region

CLASSIFICATION
Highland (Southern)

ORIGINS AND BACKGROUND
The distillery stands on the site of a 17th-century Blackford Brewery in a hollow beneath the Ochil hills and takes its name from the moor of Tullibardine, on which the nearby Gleneagles Hotel was built. The plentiful supplies of particularly good water for brewing ale (for which the old brewery at Blackford was noted) are now utilised by the distillery. The distillery was designed by Mr W. Delme Evans in 1949 for Wm S. Scott Ltd, but was acquired by Brodie Hepburn Ltd, and subsequently sold to Invergordon Distillers Ltd in 1972. Two years later, in 1974, after considerable rebuilding, the distillery's capacity was doubled. Most is used for blending, but some is also bottled as a single malt. Now part of the Whyte & Mackay group since 1993 and currently mothballed.

OWNED BY
Whyte & Mackay Distillers Ltd

VISITORS
No

AGE AND STRENGTH WHEN BOTTLED
10 years at 40% volume

COMMENTS
This is light, fresh, and clean, more resembling a Lowland malt whisky perhaps, but with a good aftermath and making a pleasant predinner dram.

RECENT CLOSURES

In recent years the following distilleries have irrevocably closed, but occasional bottles may still be available from time to time through independent bottlers.

Banff *(Banff, Banffshire. Grampian Region)*
Closed in 1983 and demolished by DCL.

Benromach *(Forres, Morayshire. Grampian Region)*
Dismantled in the 1980s by DCL.

Ben Wyvis *(Invergordon. Highland Region)*
Built next to the grain complex in 1965 and dismantled by Invergordon Distillers in 1975.

Bladnoch *(1 mile southeast of Wigtown. Dumfries & Galloway Region)*
Southernmost distillery. Closed in 1993. Sold in 1994 by United Distillers to Coordinated Developments Ltd.

Convalmore *(Dufftown. Grampian Region)*
Built in 1894. Closed by DCL in the 1980s and now used for storage by Wm Grant & Sons.

Dallas Dhu *(2 miles south of Forres. Grampian Region)*
Closed by United Distillers in 1983 and reopened as a museum showing the workings of a traditional distillery.

Glen Albyn *(Inverness. Highland Region)*
Closed by DCL in 1983 and since demolished.

Glenlochy *(Fort William. Highland Region)*
Closed by DCL in 1983 and subsequently dismantled and sold by United Distillers.

Glen Mohr *(Inverness. Highland Region)*
Next to Glen Albyn, also demolished by DCL.

Glenugie *(Peterhead, Aberdeenshire. Grampian Region)*
The most easterly distillery, it was closed by Long John International in 1982 and the machinery sold for scrap.

Glenury Royal *(Stonehaven. Grampian Region)*
Closed by DCL in 1985 and soon to be dismantled by United Distillers.

Kinclaith *(Near Glasgow. Strathclyde Region)*
In operation for only 18 years, the distillery was dismantled in 1975 by Long John International.

Ladyburn *(Girvan. Strathclyde Region)*
Built by Wm Grant & Sons next to the grain complex in 1965. It was dismantled in 1975.

Milburn *(Inverness. Highland Region)*
Closed and dismantled in 1985 by DCL, the site is now occupied by a restaurant.

North Port *(Brechin. Grampian Region)*
Closed by DCL in 1983 and subsequently dismantled and sold by United Distillers.

Port Ellen *(Port Ellen, Islay)*
This distillery was closed in the 1980s by DCL and is soon to be dismantled by United Distillers.

St Magdalene *(Linlithgow, West Lothian. Lothian Region)*
Closed down in 1983 by DCL, the site was developed into flats.

Chapter Four

Some Notable Vatted Malts

Anderson & Shaw, Ltd, founded in Glasgow in 1869, now owned by J. Deans & Co, Ltd, market Duncraggan Pure Malt.

Bartels, Rawlings International Ltd, of London, mainly known for their London Dry Gin and Barvok Vodka, also produce His Excellency Pure Malt at 5 and 12 years.

Benmore Distilleries Ltd, a subsidiary of United Distillers, market Benmore Pure Malt.

Berry Bros & Rudd, Ltd, well-known 18th-century St. James's Street wine merchants even better known for their world-famous Cutty Sark blend, also market Berry's Highland Malt, Berry's Pot Still Liqueur and All Malt.

W. Brown & Sons, Ltd, of Glasgow, whisky blenders for many years, produce Glen Stuart Pure Malt.

James Buchanan & Co., Ltd, a subsidiary of the United Distillers, market Strathconan Vatted 12-year-old Malt.

Bulloch Lade, Ltd, part of United Distillers, market the well-known Glen Ila Vatted Malt.

Burn Stewart market Glen Blair Pure Malt.

P & J Campbell, of Tomintoul, market Campbell's Tomintoul Special 100% Vatted Malt.

Cockburn & Campbell, Ltd., of London, market their Special Malt.

Cockburn & Co., Leith, founded in 1796 and now owned by The Drambuie Liquor Co., Ltd, market Cockburn's Pure Highland Malt.

M. J. Dowdeswell & Co., Ltd, based in Bristol since 1974, market Pig's Nose 4-year-old and Sheep Dip 8-year-old Pure Malt (The Original Oldbury Sheep Dip).

Findlater Mackie Todd & Co., Ltd, based in London, market Mar Lodge 8-year-old Vatted Malt.

Fine Fare, the supermarket chain, sells its own Fine Fare 12-year-old Pure Malt.

Gilbey Vintners Ltd, a subsidiary of International Distillers & Vintners, produce Strathspey Vatted Malt.

A. Gillies & Co., Ltd, a subsidiary of Barton International plc, market Royal Culross 8 years old.

Glen Burn Blenders Ltd, London, market a vatted malt Greatness.

Gordon & McPhail, of Elgin, market Old Elgin Malt, Pride of Islay 12 years old, Pride of the Lowlands 12 years old, Pride of Orkney 12 years old, Pride of Strathspey 12 years old, MacPhail's Pure Malt.

John Haig & Co., Ltd, now part of United Distillers, best known for Dimple Haig, also market Glenleven 12-year-old Vatted Malt.

Hall & Bramley Ltd, established 1860 in Liverpool as wine and spirit merchants, market Glen Carren 8-year-old Malt.

Hedges & Butler, a Bass subsidiary, market Hedges & Butler Royal Malt.

Invergordon Distillers Ltd, through their Longman subsidiary, market Glen Eagle Vatted Malt and Glen Sloy Vatted Malt.

Justerini & Brooks, Ltd, founded in the mid-18th century, now part of International Distillers & Vintners, market J & B 20-year-old Finest Malt.

Kinross Whisky Co., Ltd, based in Sussex, market Glen Baren.

The Loch Skaig Trading Co., Ltd, based in Surrey, market Old Loch Skaig 8-year-old Malt.

Lombard Scotch Whisky, Ltd, based on the Isle of Man, market Lombard's 12-year-old Pure Malt.

Andrew Macdonald (London), Ltd, based in Piccadilly, market Macdonald's Black Label 10-year-old Vatted Malt.

R. N. MacDonald & Co., Ltd, owned by Highland Stag Whiskies based in Surrey, market Glencoe 100% proof 8-year-old Highland Malt.

Macleay Duff (Distillers) Ltd, of Glasgow, market The Mill Burn 12-year-old Pure Malt.

James Martin & Co., Ltd, owned by Macdonald Martin Distilleries plc, market Dalvegan Old Highland Malt 10 years old (mostly abroad).

John Milroy Ltd, of Greek Street, London, market Milroy's 8-year-old Malt Whisky.

Mitchell Brothers of Glasgow, part of United Distillers, market Glen Dew 5-year-old Highland Malt.

Montrose Whisky Co., Ltd, London-based, market Old Montrose Pure Malt.

George Morton, Ltd, Montrose-based subsidiary of Allied Distillers, market Copper Pot 8-year-old Pure Malt.

Oakfield Ltd, of Glasgow, market Oakfield 10-year-old Malt.

Paisley Whisky Co., Ltd, based in Ayr, market Glen Garrett and Strathayr.

Praban na Linne, Ltd., on the Isle of Skye, market Poit Dhubh, pronounced *potch dhu*, Gaelic for black pot, an illicit still.

Red Lion Blending Co., Ltd, through subsidiary Douglas Denham Ltd, produce Diners 15-year-old Vatted Malt for Diners Club Inc.

Peter J. Russell & Co., Ltd, of Edinburgh, market The Seven Stills 100% Malt 5 years old, and through their subsidiary William Maxwell, Ltd, Maxwell Malt.

J. Sainsbury Ltd, the well-known grocery chain, market Sainsbury's Highland Malt 12 years old.

Seagram Distillers plc, market The Keith Classic.

R. B. Smith & Son, of Perth, market Ghillie 8-year-old Vatted Malt.

H. Stenham, Ltd, of London, through subsidiary Highland Shippers, market Highland Brook and Highlander Straight Malt and through Premier Scotch Whisky Co., Glenberry Straight Malt.

J & G Stewart, Ltd, of Edinburgh, a United Distillers subsidiary, market Ushers Old Vatted Scotch.

Duncan Taylor & Co., Ltd, of Glasgow, market Prime Malt.

Tesco, the well-known superstore, market their own Tesco Malt.

The Waverly Group, Ltd, subsidiary of Scottish & Newcastle Breweries plc, through subsidiary Christopher & Co., Ltd, market Christopher's 8-year-old Pure Malt.

Whigham Fergusson Ltd, based in Tooley Street, London, market Whigham's 12-year-old Vatted Malt.

Whigham's of Ayr Ltd, no longer associated with Whigham Fergusson, market Duart Castle Malt.

William Whiteley & Co., of London, a subsidiary of Pernod Ricard, through their Glenforres Glenlivet Distillery Co., market Glenforres 12-year-old Vatted Malt.

Chapter Five
An Almanack of Distilling Dates and Events

800 B.C.	Arrack known to have been distilled in India.
584 B.C.	Aristotle is born; later writes of distilling in his *Meteorology.*
A.D. 432	St Patrick, a native of Scotland, is sent to Wicklow to spread Christianity and also is reputed to have introduced distilling.
1494	Entry in Exchequer Rolls regarding Friar Cor making aqua vitae from malted barley by order of the King.
1498	Lord High Treasurer's Account "To the barbour that brocht aqua vitae to the King in Dundee."
1505	Barber surgeons in Edinburgh are granted right of making aqua vitae.
1506	Treasurer's accounts in Inverness mention "aqua vite to the King."
1527	*The vertuose boke of Distyllacyon* by Hieronymous Braunschweig published in English, translated by L. Andrew. First book on the subject, treats aqua vitae as a medicine.
1559	*Treasures of Evonymous,* published by Peter Morwyng, details methods of distilling process.

1579	First Act in Scotland specifically relating to aqua vitae.
1618	John Taylor in his *Pennyless Pilgrimage* visits the Earl of Mar and drinks aqua vitae.
	Earliest reference to "uisge" being drunk at a Highland chieftain's funeral.
1644	Charles I passes an Act of Excyse on "everie pynt of aquavytie or strong watteris sold within the country."
1655	R. Hage is accused of distilling on the Sabbath in St Ninian's Kirk session records.
1675	Boyle rediscovers the principle of the hydrometer.
1690	Ferintosh first distillery mentioned by name. Forbes of Culloden, who had "suffered the loss of his brewery of aqua vitae by fire in his absence" in 1689 fighting for William of Orange against James, is granted freedom from excise duty.
1707	Act of Union of Parliaments is passed against much opposition, specifically excluding a tax on malt in Scotland.
1715	Attempt to introduce Malt Tax in Scotland withdrawn.
1725	Malt taxed in Scotland and riots result.
1726	In his *Letters* Captain Burt, an English engineer in the Highlands, refers to the Highlanders drinking whisky "like water."
1736	Gin Act in England aimed at checking consumption causes open flouting of law at height of Gin Era.
1745	Prince Charles raises standard at Glenfinnan.
1746	Prince Charles defeated at Culloden and flees country.
1747	Lt. Col. Watson in Fort Augustus advises his officers to get the Highlanders "drunk with whisky."
1751	An Act of Parliament specifically ends Scotland's exemption from taxation so that it is no longer advantageous to import spirits from Scotland.
1784	The Wash Act defines the Highland Line by Act of Parliament.
1786	Distillery Act introduces Licensing system at

prompting of English gin lobby. Duty raised in Scotland to English level. No distinction between Highlands and Lowlands. This unfairness results in much illicit distilling.

1788 Duty increased. Stein brothers are bankrupted.

1793 Tax on whisky trebled to £9.

1795 Tax on whisky doubled to £18. Some stills operate continuously to beat tax.

1797 Tax trebled to £54.

1800 Tax doubled again to £108.

1805 Tax is raised yet again to £162.

The firm of Seager Evans is formed in London to make gin.

1814 Stills under 500 gallons forbidden in the Highlands, which General Stewart of Garth says amounts to a complete interdict.

Matthew Gloag sets up as a whisky merchant in Perth.

1815 The output of the distillery at Drumin in Glenlivet run by George Smith, grandson of John Smith Gow, was already a hogshead a week. Due to the pure water and fine peat available, the illicit whisky distilled there is regarded as the finest in Scotland and is drunk by many Highland lairds including Grant of Rothiemurchus, MP, and a lawyer in Edinburgh.

1817 Teaninich distillery is built by Captain H. Munro in Ross-shire.

1818 Bladnoch distillery is founded near Wigtown by the Maclelland family.

1819 Clynelish distillery near Brora is built by Marquis of Stafford.

1820 John Walker sets up as a licensed grocer in Kilmarnock.

1821 Linkwood distillery near Elgin is built.

1822 George IV visits Scotland and is provided with illicitly distilled Glenlivet whisky from Grant of Rothiemurchus.

1823 A new act introduces a £10 License fee and duty of 2s 3d per gallon of whisky distilled.

	Springbank distillery near Campbeltown is founded by farmers named Mitchell.
1824	At the prompting of his landlord, the Duke of Gordon, George Smith takes out the first license under the new act as the first legal distillery in Glenlivet.
1825	T. R. Sandeman starts as a whisky merchant in Perth.
1826	Robert Stein patents his single-distillation still.
	Tax raised to 2s 10d per proof gallon.
1830	Tax per proof gallon raised to 3s 6d.
	Stein builds his first patent-still at Kirkliston.
	Talisker is founded on the Isle of Skye.
1831	Aeneas Coffey invents his patent-still making grain whisky by continuous distillation.
	Justerini and Brooks enter into partnership in London.
1832	The Glen Scotia distillery is founded in Campbeltown by Stewart Galbraith.
1836	The Glanfarclas distillery is founded by Robert Hay.
1838	Hill Thomson whisky merchants are granted Royal Warrant.
1840	Glen Grant distillery is built at Rothes by James and John Grant.
	Glenkinchie distillery is founded in E. Lothian by J. Gray.
	Tax per proof gallon is raised to 3s 8d.
1841	James Chivas starts as merchant in Aberdeen.
1842	Glenmorangie distillery starts at Tain by William Mathieson.
1846	John Dewar starts as wine and spirit merchant in Perth.
1848	Queen Victoria and family visit John Begg at Lochnagar distillery.
1853	Andrew Usher is credited with producing the first blended whisky.
	Gladstone raises the tax to 4s 8d per proof gallon.
1854	Crimean War. Tax raised to 6s per proof gallon.

1855	Tax raised to 8s per proof gallon.
1856	First Trade Arrangement by Grain Distillers.
	Tax raised by 1d per proof gallon.
1857	W. & A. Gilbey set up as wine and spirit merchants.
	William Thomson joins William Hill and forms Hill Thomson as whisky merchants at 45 Frederick Street, Edinburgh.
1860	Gladstone raises the tax to 10s per proof gallon.
1865	Glenfarclas distillery is bought by John Grant of Blairfindy.
	Whisky merchants Menzies, Barnard & Craig, John Bald & Co., John Haig & Co., NacNab Bros, Robert Mowbray, and Macfarlane & Co. form their first Trade Arrangement.
1870	*Phylloxera vastatrix* begins to attack the French vineyards.
1874	The North of Scotland Malt Distillers Association is formed.
1877	The Distillers Company Ltd is formed by the whisky merchants who had formed a Trade Arrangement in 1865, with Menzies, Barnard & Craig replaced by Stewart & Co.
	John Haig founds his company at Markinch in Fife.
1880	John Walker opens a London office.
	Colonel John Gordon Smith, son of George Smith, goes to court on the subject of the use of the name Glenlivet. It is held that he is the only one entitled to the name "The Glenlivet"; everyone else must use it as an affix to their own distillery name.
1881	Bruichladdich Islay Malt distillery is founded.
1882	William Sanderson produces his blend Vat 69.
	James Whyte and Charles Mackay found Whyte & Mackay Ltd.
1884	James Buchanan sets up in London with the blend Black & White.
	William Shaw at Hill Thomson produces the blend Queen Anne.

1886	DCL shares are quoted on London Stock Exchange.
1887	The Glenfiddich distillery is built by William Grant.
	The Dufftown-Glenlivet distillery is founded.
	Highland Distilleries is formed to acquire the Islay distillery of William Grant and the Glenrothes-Glenlivet distillery.
1888	The North British grain distillery is founded with a productive capacity of 3 million gallons per annum in opposition to the growing power of the DCL.
	Mackie & Co. take over the Lagavulin distillery on Islay for White Horse.
1891	Balvenie distillery is founded by William Grant of Glenfiddich.
1893	Cardow is bought by John Walker.
1894	Longmorn-Glenlivet is built by Longmorn Co.
1895	Aultmore is built by Alexander Edward of Sanquhar, Forres.
1896	John Dewar builds a distillery at Aberfeldy.
1898	The Pattison brothers go bankrupt, ending the whisky boom.
1900	The tax per proof gallon is raised to 11s.
1906	Islington Borough Council brings the "What is whisky?" case. Basically malt v. grain. DCL presses for Royal Commission when verdict in favour of malt.
1908	A Royal Commission on Whisky decides grain and malt blended make Scotch whisky.
1909	Lloyd George raises the tax per proof gallon to 14s 9d.
1914	First World War.
	Scottish Malt Distillers forms as DCL subsidiary.
1915	Central Liquor Control Board is formed.
	Immature Spirits Act requires two years' compulsory bonding.
1916	Compulsory bonding extended to three years.
1917	Dilution of Proof to 30 under proof.
	Whisky Association is formed.

1918	War ends.
	Bonar Law increases tax by 15s 3d to 30s.
1919	Chamberlain increases tax per proof gallon to 50s.
1920	Prohibition is introduced in USA.
	Chamberlain increases tax to 72s 6d per proof gallon.
1924	John Haig merges with DCL.
1925	Buchanan-Dewars and John Walker merge with DCL, with William Ross of DCL as Chairman.
1926	The Pot-Still Malt Distillers Association is formed in place of the North of Scotland Malt Distillers Association to include all malt distillers.
1927	Seager Evans sets up Strathclyde distillery for grain whisky.
	White Horse Distillers is acquired by the DCL.
1928	The Distillers Co. of Canada takes over Seagrams and Sons.
1929	Wall Street crash and depression.
1930	Hiram Walker of Ontario acquires Glenburgie-Glenlivet.
1932	Prohibition is repealed by President F. D. Roosevelt.
1933	Arthur Bell & Sons acquires the Blair-Athol and Dufftown-Glenlivet distilleries.
1936	Edward VIII abdicates. George VI succeeds. Hiram Walker acquires George Ballantine & Co., of Dum-barton; also Milton-Duff distillery.
	Arthur Bell & Sons acquires the Inchgower distillery near Fochabers.
	Seager Evans acquires John Long.
1937	Seager Evans takes over Glenugie distillery at Peterhead.
1938	Hiram Walker opens a £3 million grain distillery at Inverleven, Dumbarton.
1939	Second World War.
	Tax per proof gallon is raised by 10s to 82s 6d.
	Grain distilling halts, limited pot-still malt distilling is permitted.

1940 Tax per proof gallon raised by 15s to 97s 6d.

1942 Tax per proof gallon raised by 40s to 137s 6d.

1945 End of 1939–45 War.

1947 Tax raised by 33s 4d to 190s 10d by Hugh Dalton.

1948 Tax raised by 20s to 210s 10d by Stafford Cripps.

1950 Seagrams takes over Strathisla distillery.

1952 George IV is succeeded by Elizabeth II.

George & J. G. Smith Ltd and J. & J. Grant Glen Grant Ltd form The Glenlivet & Glen Grant Distillers Ltd.

1954 Hiram Walker takes over Glencadam distillery in Brechin and Scapa distillery in Orkney.

1955 Hiram Walker takes over Pulteney distillery in Wick.

1956 Seager Evans is bought by Schenley Industries of New York, in turn owned by the Glen Alden Corporation.

1957 Seager Evans builds Kinclaith distillery near Glasgow.

1958 Seager Evans builds a new distillery at Tormore on the Spey, north of Grantown-on-Spey.

1959 Inver House, an American-owned company, a subsidiary of Publicker Industries, Inc., builds a new grain distillery by Airdrie and an associated Lowland malt distillery named Glenflagler.

1960 The Scotch Whisky Association is incorporated to provide legal status in foreign courts.

Glenfarclas distillery is doubled in size.

Ledaig distillery is founded in Tobermory.

Jura distillery is started by Scottish & Newcastle Breweries, Ltd.

1961 The tax per proof gallon raised by 21s to 231s 10d.

1962 Seager Evans acquires Laphroaig.

W & A Gilbey, Gilbey Twiss, Justerini & Brooks, and United Vintners form International Distillers and Vintners Ltd.

1964 The tax per proof gallon is raised to £12.87.

1965	The tax per proof gallon is raised to £14.60.
	Caperdonich and Benriach distilleries are rebuilt after having been silent for over 60 years.
	Invergordon Distillers Ltd is formed.
1966	The tax per proof gallon is raised to £16.06.
	Tamnavulin-Glenlivet distillery is built by Invergordon Distillers Ltd, on the banks of the River Livet.
1968	The tax per proof gallon is raised to £17.14 in March and to £18.85 in November.
1969	Glen Alden Corporation, who owned Schenley Industries, who owned Seager Evans, is taken over by Rapid American Incorporated. The name Seager Evans is changed to Long John International Ltd.
1970	The Glenlivet & Glen Grant Distilleries Ltd merges with Hill Thomson & Co. Ltd and Longmorn-Glenlivet Distilleries Ltd.
	Amalgamated Distilled Products Ltd is formed with the Campbeltown Glen Scotia distillery and other interests.
	The Highland Distillers Co. Ltd acquires Matthew Gloag Ltd.
1971	Chivas Bros, the Scots subsidiary of Seagrams, begins plans for a distillery in Glenlivet.
	Currency is decimalised in Britain.
1972	The Glenlivet & Glen Grant Distilleries Ltd rationalise their name to The Glenlivet Distillers Ltd.
	The Pot-Still Malt Distillers Association of Scotland rationalise their name to The Malt Distillers Association of Scotland.
	Watney, Mann & Co. Ltd acquires International Distillers & Vintners Ltd.
	Whyte & Mackay Distillers Ltd, Dalmore, and Tomintoul distilleries are acquired by Scottish & Universal Investments Ltd.
1973	Britain enters the European Economic Community.
	With the introduction of VAT, the duty on whisky is reduced for the first time since 1896.

Bladnoch distillery is sold by Inver House Distillers to Arthur Bell & Sons.

Grand Metropolitan acquires Watney, Mann & Co. Ltd, hence International Distillers & Vintners Ltd.

Braes of Glenlivet distillery starts operations.

1974 The Glenlivet Distillers Ltd 150th anniversary since George Smith first took out a licence in 1824.

The Malt Distillers of Scotland centenary.

Lonrho acquires Scottish & Universal Investments Ltd, hence also Whyte & Mackay Distillers Ltd.

Pernod Ricard acquires House of Campbell and control of Aberlour distillery.

1975 Whitbread acquires Long John International.

Allt-a-Bhainne distillery starts production for Seagram Distillers Ltd.

1976 Seagram Distillers Ltd opens a vatting and blending complex at Keith with a capacity of 3½ million gallons per annum.

1978 Seagram acquires The Glenlivet Distillers Ltd.

1980 Heineken acquires 20% of Tomatin Distillers plc.

1981 Ben Nevis Distillery is acquired by Long John International.

1982 Pernod Ricard acquires William Whiteley and control of Edradour distillery.

1983 DCL closes 11 of their 45 distilleries, including Banff, Benromach, Brora, Dallas Dhu, Glen Albyn, Glenochy, Glen Mohr, North Port, Knockdhu, Port Ellen, and St Magdalene. Banff, Glen Mohr, and Glen Albyn in Inverness are subsequently demolished. Dallas Dhu reopens in 1988 as a museum. St Magdalene in Linlithgow has been turned into flats.

1985 Invergordon Distillers acquires Mackinlay and control of Jura and Glenallachie distilleries from Scottish & Newcastle Breweries.

Glenugie Distillery is dismantled and sold.

1986 Arthur Bell & Sons plc is acquired by Guinness plc after lengthy takeover battle.

1987	Tomatin distillery is acquired by a Japanese consortium, Takara Shuzo & Okura & Co. Ltd.
	Guinness plc acquires control of DCL after allegedly fraudulent transactions in bitter takeover battle. It is agreed that HQ will be based in Scotland.
	Long John International is renamed James Burroughs Distillers.
1988	The Nikka Company of Japan is acquired by Ben Nevis Distillery from Long John International and plans to restart distilling in 1990.
	Management buyout at Invergordon Distillers.
	Allied-Lyons plc acquires Hiram Walker and Allied-Distillers Ltd is formed, including George Ballantine & Son, William Teacher & Sons, and Stewart & Son of Dundee.
	Whyte & Mackay sold by Lonrho to Brent Walker. DCL is merged with Arthur Bell & Sons plc, and is renamed United Distillers plc. The headquarters to remain in London despite repeated assurances to the contrary during takeover and subsequently.
	Control of Barton International plc., part of the Argyll Group, owners of Littlemill and Glen Scotia Distilleries, passed to Schenley International (Canada) plc, but later, following a management buyout, is renamed Gibson International plc.
1989	Suntory holding in Macallan raised to 12%.
	Remy Martin own 11% in Macallan.
	Ardbeg distillery is reopened by Allied Distillers and Imperial and Glentauchers acquired from United Distillers plc, to be reopened.
	Management buyout at Morrison Bowmore Distillers, owners of Bowmore, Auchentoshan, and Glengarioch distilleries. Suntory has 35% holding. The Scotch Whisky Heritage Centre opens in Castlehill, Edinburgh, with superb audiovisual displays, showing the history of Scotch whisky and the various stages of the whisky distilling process. 58% owned by American Brands Inc.

1990 Whitbread, owners of Long John International Ltd, James Burroughs Distillers, sell Tormore and Laphroaig distilleries to Allied Distillers Ltd.

Seagram Distillers Ltd sell 45 Frederick Street, Edinburgh, the group and Hill Thomson headquarters since 1857, 133 years after it was established as their base.

Gallaghers Tobacco plc take over Whyte & Mackay.

Kininvie distillery comes on-stream.

1991 Whyte & Mackay, subsidiary of U.S.-based Gallagher Group, gain 42% shareholding in Invergordon Distillers after a hard-fought takeover battle.

The Speyside Distillery comes on-stream.

Burn Stewart & Co. Ltd of Glasgow acquire Deanston from Invergordon for £2.1 million.

1992 EEC standards accepted. The standard size of bottle changes from 75 cl to 70 cl. It is decreed that Scotch whisky shall only be distilled and produced in Scotland at no less than 40% volume, otherwise it is impossible to check where it has been distilled.

Inver House Distillers Ltd buy the Speyburn distillery from United Distillers.

In his March budget, Chancellor Norman Lamont raises the duty on whisky by 85p to £19.81 per proof litre. The Exchequer now receives £5.54 in duty for each 70 cl bottle of whisky sold in Britain.

1993 Whyte & Mackay Group acquire Invergordon Distillers for U.S.-based conglomerate American Brands Inc., which owns Gallagher Ltd.

Burn Stewart Distillers plc acquire Tobermory.

Bladnoch permanently closed by United Distillers.

1994 Tobermory comes on-stream.

Control of Morrison Bowmore passed to Suntory, who now have a considerable stake in the industry in Scotland as well as in Japan.

VAT is raised to 17.5%, compounding taxation.

Chancellor Kenneth Clarke raises duty on whisky

by 26p a bottle in emergency budget despite protests from the industry.

1995 Whyte & Mackay mothball Bruichladdich, Tamnavoulin, and Tullibardine distilleries because of overproduction following the budget tax rise.

Inver House acquire Pulteney from Allied.

After around a £30 million loss of revenue, Chancellor Kenneth Clarke removes 27p per bottle tax on spirits in his autumn budget.

Glossary of Technical Terms

Diastase In the process of germination the embryo of the barley secretes diastase, which makes the starch in the barley soluble and breaks it down. This is then checked by drying.

Draff The grain left in the mash tun after the wort has been drawn off for distilling. It is widely used as cattle food and is one of the by-products of the distilling process.

Drying shed With its typical pagoda-shaped ventilators, the drying shed, where the malted barley is dried, is one of the established features of the older distilleries in Scotland.

Feints This is the third part of the distilled spirit in the second distillation of the pot-still distilling process. It consists of the undesirable higher alcohols. They are generally re-distilled.

Foreshots These are the first part of the distilled spirit in the second distillation of the pot-still distilling process. They consist of the undesirable lower alcohols. The "middle cut," which follows, is the desirable spirit used to make malt whisky.

Highland Line Introduced by Act of Parliament in 1784 to define for tax purposes the difference between Highland and Lowland distillers. If the Line were applicable today, most of the Banffshire and Aberdeen distilleries would be considered Lowland.

Low wines This is the product of the first part of the pot-still distilling process. It is the product of the distilled wash. The feints and foreshots are generally added to this prior to the second distilling process.

Malt Barley (or other grain) prepared for brewing or distilling by steeping, germinating, and kiln drying.

Mash The dried malted barley is ground in a mill and then mixed with boiling water in a circular container known as the mash tun. The soluble starch is then turned into a sugary liquid called wort.

Middle cut The desirable spirit produced between the foreshots and the feints in the pot-still process.

On-stream A distillery comes "on-stream" when distilling starts.

Patent-still Also known as the Coffey Still, after its inventor Aeneas Coffey. Also known as a continuous still, since it works continuously producing grain whisky, unlike the two separate operations of the pot-still.

Pot-still A large, usually round-sided, copper vessel used for the distillation of malt whisky. There are two pot-stills required for the process: firstly the wash-still, which produces low wines. These are then distilled in the adjoining smaller spirit-still, which produces malt whisky.

Proof This is the technical term by which the strength of the spirit produced is measured. One of the early methods used was to mix the spirit with gunpowder and light it. If the powder lit there was deemed to be enough spirit to allow it to do so and this was then known as "proved." If there was no flash the spirit was held to be too weak. Today, using a Sikes

Hydrometer the strength is accurately measured.

Proof spirit Under the 1952 Customs & Excise Act "Spirits shall be deemed to be at proof if the volume of the ethyl alcohol contained therein made up to the volume of the spirits with distilled water has a weight equal to that of twelve-thirteenths of a volume of distilled water equal to the volume of the spirits, the volume of each liquid being computed as at 51 degrees Fahrenheit."

Saccharify To convert into sugar. In the distilling process this arises between malting and mash tun when the diastase enzyme turns the starch in the grain into sugar.

Single whisky Either malt or grain whisky produced by a single distillery.

Single-single Either malt or grain whisky produced from a single distillation by a single distillery.

Uisge Beatha The Gaelic for *eau de vie* or water of life. Used to refer to spirit distilled from malted barley, it was shortened to "uisge," or "usky," hence the origin of the word whisky.

Wash The term used for the liquid obtained from fermented wort. This is used for the first pot-still distillation process or for the patent-still.

Wort The liquid drawn from the mash tun containing the sugar from the malted barley. With the addition of yeast it is then fermented prior to being distilled as wash.

Zern A Transatlantic term for a measure of Scotch malt whisky; a sufficient quantity taken after any sporting activity to repel any chill and induce reflective discussion of the day; hence, a Zernful.

Further Reading: A Bibliography of Scotch

Barnard, Alfred. *The Whisky Distilleries of the United Kingdom* (Harper, 1887).

Bell, Colin. *Scotch Whisky* (Lang Syne Publishers, 1954).

Brander, Michael. *The Original Scotch* (Hutchinson, London, 1974).

________. *A Guide to Scotch Whisky* (Johnston & Bacon, 1975).

________. *An Introduction to Scotch Whisky* (Spurbooks, 1982).

________. *The Essential Guide to Scotch Whisky* (Canongate, 1990).

Bruce-Lockhart, Sir Robert. *Scotch* (Putnam, 1959).

Cooper, Derek. *A Taste of Scotch* (Deutsch, 1989).

________. *A Guide to the Whiskies of Scotland* (Pitman, 1981).

________. *The Century Companion to Whiskies* (Century, 1987).

Cooper, Derek and Fay Godwin. *The Whisky Roads of Scotland* (Norman & Hobhouse, 1982).

Cooper, Derek and Dione Patullo. *Enjoying Scotch* (Cassel, 1980).

Daiches, David. *Scotch Whisky: Past & Present* (Collins).

________. *Scotch Whisky* (Deutsch, 1969).

________. *Let's Collect Scotch Whisky* (Jarrold).

Dunnett, Alastair. *The Land of Scotch* (S.W.A., 1953).

Fleming, Susan. *The Little Whisky Book* (Piatkus, 1991).

Gunn, Neil M. *Whisky and Scotland* (Routledge, 1935).

Hallgarten, Peter. *Spirits & Liqueurs* (Faber & Faber, 1979).

Hastings, Derek. *Spirits and Liqueurs of the World* (Apple, 1984).

House, Jack. *The Pride of Perth: A History of Arthur Bell & Sons* (Hutchinson Benham, 1976).

House, Jack, with Theodora FitzGibbon, S. Russell Grant, Donald Mackinlay, High MacDiarmid, Bill Simpson, and Anthony Troon. *Scotch Whisky* (Macmillan, 1979).

Hume, James R. See Moss.
Jackson, Michael. *Malt Whisky* (Dorling Kindersley, 1989).
_______. *The World Guide to Whisky* (Dorling Kindersley).
_______. *A Guide to Scotch Whisky* (1988).
Keegan, Alan. *Scotch in Miniature* (Famedrame, 1976).
Lamond, John. *Scotland's Malt Distilleries* (Benedict Books, 1989).
Laver, James. *The House of Haig* (1958).
Lord, Tony. *The World Guide to Spirits, Liqueurs, Aperitifs and Cocktails* (Macdonald & Janes, 1979).
MacDonald, Aeneas. *Whisky* (Porpoise Press, 1950).
Mackie, Albert D. *The Scotch Whisky Drinker's Companion* (Ramsay Head Press, 1975).
McDowall, R. J. S. *The Whiskies of Scotland* (John Murray, 1967).
Milroy, Wallace. *Malt Whisky Almanac* (Lochar, 1986).
Morrice, Philip. *The Schweppes Guide to Scotch* (Alphabooks, 1983).
_______. *The Whisky Distilleries of Scotland and Ireland* (Harper).
Moss, Michael S. and James R. Hume. *The Making of Scotch Whisky* (James & James).
Murphy, Brian. *The World Book of Whisky* (Collins, 1978).
Robb, J. Marshall. *Scotch Whisky* (W & R Chambers, 1950).
Ross, James. *Whisky* (Routledge, 1970).
Saintsbury, George. *Notes on a Cellar Book* (Macmillan, 1920).
Sillett, S. W. *Illicit Scotch* (Beaver Books, 1965).
Simon, Andre. *Drink* (Burke Publishing, 1948).
Skipton, Mark. *The Scotch Whisky Book* (Hamlyn, 1980).
Stenekey, Fred. *Whisky: The Complete Whisky Book* (Collins, 1980).
Targett, David and Raymond K. Ashton. *Scotch Whisky: Too Much or Too Little* (Tomatin Distillers, Co., Ltd., 1981).
Taylor, Iain Cameron. *Highland Whisky:* (An Comunn Caidhealach, 1968).
Weir, Ronald B. *A History of the Pot Still Malt Distillers' Association* (Elgin, 1970).
Wilson, John. *Scotland's Malt Whiskies* (Famedrame, 1975).
_______. *Scotland's Distilleries: A Visitor's Guide* (Famedrame).
Wilson, Neil. *Scotch & Water* (Lochar Publishing).
Wilson, Ross. *Scotch Made Easy* (Hutchinson, 1959).
_______. *Scotch* (Constable, 1970).
_______. *Scotch, Its History and Romance* (David & Charles, 1973).